Mystical Poems of Jnaneshwar

AF539898

Mystical Poems of Jnaneshwar

ANAND MUNDRA

Original Translations from the Marathi

MYSTICAL POEMS OF JNANESHWAR

First Edition : Delhi, 2019

© Anand Mundra
All Rights Reserved

ISBN : 978 81 940111 2 5

MOTILAL BANARSIDASS PUBLICATIONS
93, Shyam Lal Marg, Darya Ganj, New Delhi-110002

Cover and illustrations design by Neeraja Mathur
Editing and interior design by Laura Duggan
Nicasio Press Illustrations used under Creative Commons Attribution-ShareA like 4.0 International License.

MLBD Cataloging-in-Publication Data
Mystical Poems of Jnaneshwar:
Original Translation from Marathi by
Anand Mundra
ISBN : 978 81 94 0111 2 5
Includes Notes and Bibliography
I. Hinduism II. Spirituality III. Jnaneshwar
IV. Abhangas V. Mundra, Anand

Published by
MOTILAL BANARSIDASS PUBLICATIONS
www.mlbdbooks@gmail.com
Printed in by Replika Press Pvt. Ltd.

To the memory of my late father, Damodardas Mundra, who sang Jnaneshwar's songs to me when I was not yet three years old, and to my spiritual master Swami Muktananda, who much later made them all come alive in experience.

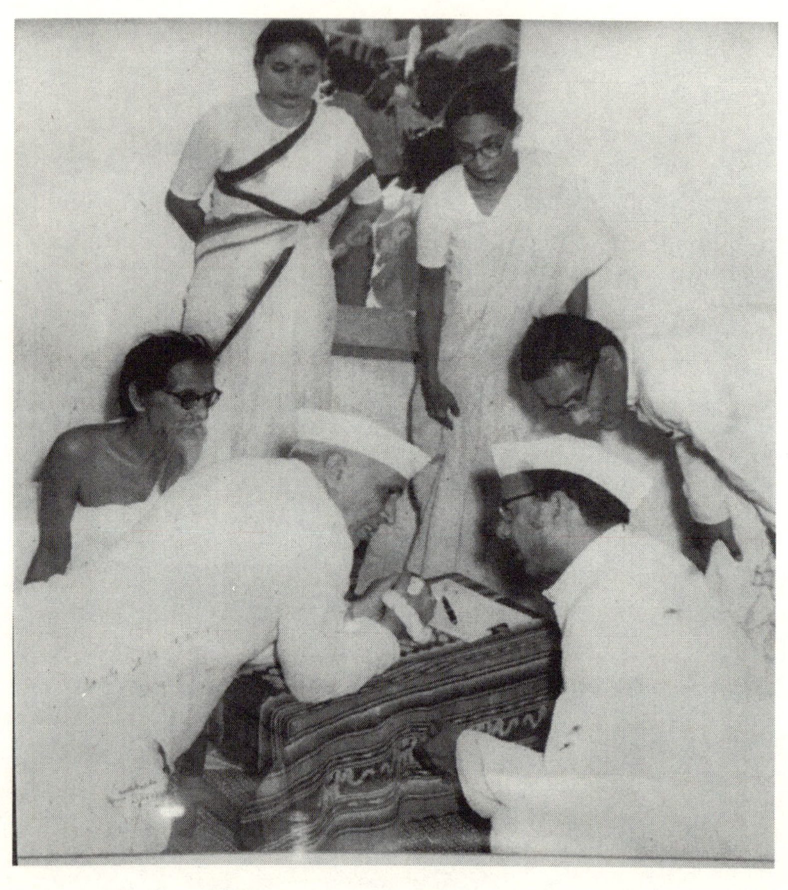

Damodardas Mundra with Acharya Vinoba Bhave and Pt. Jawaharlal Nehru

All of creation
swims in the nectar of immortality;
what a wondrous sight it is.

The world and its witness, the holy and its power,
their two-ness is reflected in you.
They make your body.

Jnandev says, look for yourself in your own body.
The whole world bears the stamp of its maker.

Damodardas Mundra with Acharya Vinoba Bhave
and Jayaprakash Narayan

ACKNOWLEDGMENTS

Although there are many to acknowledge for this labor of love, I especially wish to offer my gratitude to three people: Arundhati (Deepali) Adivarekar, my friend in Pune, India, with whom I read and worked on many of Jnaneshwar's poems for several months; my niece Neeraja Mathur for the design of the cover and other visuals; and my friend Laura Duggan, who encouraged me with this project from the beginning, and provided invaluable technical editing, design, and other guidance leading to this publication.

Damodardas Mundra and wife Meera with Pt. Nehru

Table of Contents

Translator's Preface

I learned about Jnaneshwar at my father's knees. My father, Damodardas Mundra, was Vinoba Bhave's secretary from 1945 to 1960. Vinoba was the spiritual heir to Mahatma Gandhi. Gandhi had several high-profile "disciples"— Jawaharlal Nehru, Vallabh Bhai Patel, and Vinoba, among others. As is well known, Gandhi's politics were rooted in a deep, personal spirituality—the spirituality of truth, non-violence, and service. After Gandhi, the political and spiritual portions of his legacy seemed to get divided, and all his close associates, except Vinoba, went immediately into politics. Jawaharlal Nehru became free India's first prime minister and remained so for years to come.

Vinoba, on the other hand, remembered Gandhi's insight that the real India lived in the villages, as the poor, disenfranchised, wildly-exploited lot that tilled the land and got nothing but welts on their backs from the landlords' whips for it. Like Gandhi, Vinoba was committed to putting the spiritual essence into action in the service of this exploited humanity. Vinoba walked all over India from village to village appealing to the landlords to share their land with their tenants. He collected millions of acres of land this way and distributed them to the poor. My father, as his secretary, was at the forefront of this movement, in constant contact with Vinoba for many hours a day.

An intellectual giant steeped in the spiritual heritage of India, Vinoba authored hundreds of books, speaking, writing, collating, commenting, and interpreting nearly every aspect of the Indian spiritual heritage. Of all the greats he studied and interpreted, one stood above all: Jnaneshwar. Vinoba says of Jnaneshwar: "It was Jnaneshwar that gave me my way, my feeling, my language, my inspiration. Jnaneshwar did for me what even Gandhi could not." In *Jnandevanchi Bhajane,* Vinoba said of Jnaneshwar, "There have been many; there are many; there will be many; but like unto him, there is only one: himself."

In 1949, before he started his *pada-yatra,* his travel by foot over the entire Indian continent one village at a time, Vinoba still lived in my hometown, Wardha, now in Maharashtra State in India. My father walked five miles each way many days in the week, starting his day with taking dictations from Vinoba at four in the morning. This was the time Vinoba spent studying, reading, and contemplating. Many a day, Vinoba would read *abhangas* (poems) of Jnaneshwar, sing them, become lost in contemplation, and eventually start talking about them. My father wrote these commentaries down, and then collated them. These became Vinoba's *Jnanadev Chintanika, Contemplations on Jnandev.* These were all in Marathi.

When my father wasn't at Vinoba's *ashram,* he came home to his 3-year-old son—me—and sang these poems of Jnaneshwar as lullabies to me. Later, he also translated them into Hindi.

After I met my spiritual master Swami Muktananda, I began having first-hand experiences of the divine that Jnaneshwar wrote about. Jnaneshwar's writings are full of deep mysticism, chronicling states and stages of the inner journey that can take place after a spiritual awakening. Muktananda often spoke of these stages at length, and quoted Jnaneshwar frequently and eloquently. He wrote highly accessible accounts of many of the spiritual experiences in his spiritual autobiography, *Play of Consciousness*. As I listened and read, Jnaneshwar's words came alive for me. I became seized with the desire to translate Jnaneshwar's poems.

I have been at this project now for twenty-five years, translating Jnaneshwar's poetry into English. It was a project that would not conclude itself. A few years ago, in 2014, I started going back to the city of Pune, twenty kilometers from Jnaneshwar's shrine in Alandi, and the project began to come together. Nearly every day I met someone new, yet another person who loved Jnaneshwar even more than I did, and I began to experience how he still enlivens and enlightens the lives and the pulse of this culture. I began reading with friends, who loved the project just as much as I did, because they got to spend time with his words. The translations slowly began to take shape. I finally had some 200 of his nearly 1000 poems translated, scattered in several notebooks. This book contains a selection from those 200. There are many others that remain to be translated. I only hope that I will get to the rest of them.

ABOUT THE TRANSLATIONS

I must say a word here about the approach used in the translations. Naturally, I have tried to be as faithful to the original as possible. I am fluent in both Marathi and English. However, Jnaneshwar's Marathi is to modern Marathi as old English is to modern English. Porting words across the boundaries of culture, language, time, history, tradition, and the philosophical and mystical heritage from Marathi into English is a challenging and humbling task. To add to the difficulties inherent in such porting, Jnaneshwar's poems are especially susceptible to multiple interpretations. This is not as much the case for the verses in *Jnaneshwari*; however, it is especially true of his poems, which often encapsulate a whole experience in a few words. P. N. Joshi notes this in *Saartha Sri Jnandeva Abhanga Gaathaa* and acknowledges that other interpretations are possible. We owe a note of gratitude to both Dada Maharaj Sakhare and P.N. Joshi, whose Marathi prose translations we have consulted. However, we have also deviated in many places from their interpretations, especially for verses dense with yogic stages and experiences.

Perhaps it is possible to translate the poetry literally. However, whether any of its beauty and power would survive after such translation is questionable. The frequent use of words commonplace in the Indian Hindu yogic tradition without any counterpart in English poses a deep challenge. We made a deliberate decision to make the main body as accessible to the modern contemporary Western reader/seeker as possible. Direct use of many philosophical words commonplace in India and in Marathi has been avoided, and translated in a way that hopes to approach the original intent. Notes have been provided to cite the original words in most such cases.

In spite of the intent to avoid as much of the cultural and linguistic otherness as possible, we have retained the use of certain words where we felt not using them would take away from its richness. It would be impossible not to use the appellation *Vitthal,* Jnaneshwar's chosen deity, and its numerous synonyms, Krishna, Govinda, Hari, and occasionally even Rama. Also notable is the use of

Brahman, which we have sometimes left as is, but sometimes translated simply as "the Absolute." We have often left in the word *maya,* the cosmic force or power of illusion, but sometimes used other suggestive words when we felt it would not impede the meaning. An example of words we have tried not to use is *gunas,* the three traditional "strands" that make up nature (*prakriti*) according to the Hindu tradition. Instead we have tried to use suggestive words to convey the spirit of such words. Where we have substituted plain English words for such technical terms, we have provided notes that indicate the original words or text.

Besides the beauty, emotional appeal, and directness of his expression, Jnaneshwar's poems often also combine the various aspects of his personality in a single poem: a man of knowledge, a yogi, a devotee, and sometimes a seeker. In translating his poems, it is often difficult to convey all these aspects, which exist simultaneously in the original. We sometimes had to choose an emphasis. We feel that above all, Jnaneshwar was in a state of complete union with the divine, and that perhaps the most significant aspect of his poems is that if we would be open to him, they would catapult us directly into that same experience, that same *anubhava.* Therefore, when we had to choose an emphasis, we sometimes preferred this aspect: their aspect as an *upaaya,* a tool that we ourselves could use to touch the infinite, a direct resource for the spiritual seeker. I was fortunate that in the process of translating, I was forced to sit with these poems closely and could not avoid their power. Our apologies, however, if in doing this we sometimes couldn't convey the other exquisite aspects.

In the end, Jnaneshwar's poetry speaks to the heart. His *abhangas,* poems, or *ovis,* as they are often called, have a distinct flow and music. We have tried to carry and convey some of that cadence. One only hopes that the poems touch the readers' heart enough to make them go looking for more of the treasures of this master, who was and is as important to central-western India as Rumi would be to Persia or Kabir to North India.

The poems in this book are a somewhat random sample from the *Gaatha,* his priceless collection of nearly 1000 abhangas. These are his devotional poems. There is some debate regarding the authorship of some of the poems. We find many of the arguments refuting his authorship dubious. For this manuscript, we have used the traditional and widely used *Gaathaa* compiled by Sakhare Maharaj, published as *Sakala Sant Gaathaa* (SSG) by K.A Joshi (1975). We should note, however, that SSG certainly contains typos. The compilations by Dada Maharaj Sakhare and P. N. Joshi both contain all the poems used here. There are numerous minor variations among these three regarding short or long vowels, nasals, and occasionally other issues. Although we have favored SSG, when in doubt, we consulted all three compilations and used the reading that made the most sense.

A note at the bottom of each poem provides the numbering of the poems in the source text, indicated by *SSG* and the number.

ABOUT SPELLING

In Marathi, Jnaneshwar is *Dnyaneshwar*. Jnandev is *Dnyandev*. The poems themselves often end with "*dnyandev mhane...*" meaning "Dnyandev says…". There is a deeper intimacy conveyed by *Dnyandev*. However, we have opted for *Jnaneshwar* and *Jnandev,* in deference to the wider, scholarly practice of the representation of the Marathi "*dny*" as "*jn*" in English, and the placement in

Sanskrit dictionaries. The same consideration is true for the name *Nivritti.* He is *Nivrutti* in Marathi, but we have surrendered to *Nivritti,* in deference to common practice.

All the poems have been rendered from Marathi by the author. May you enjoy them as much as millions of seekers have over the past 800 years.

Mystical Poems of Jnaneshwar

Introduction

The birth of Jnaneshwar, literally "Lord of Knowledge," was one of those events in the literary and mystical history of India that has shaped and transformed the lives of millions, and may continue to do so for centuries to come. Jnaneshwar's works have been read, recited, memorized, danced to, and revered by the Marathi-speaking population in India, which today numbers over 100 million people. Jnaneshwar's substantial body of work, created very early in the history of the Marathi language, established an indelible course for the spiritual aspiration of the Marathi-speaking people. Its imprint on the Marathi culture and language can be felt to this day.

Born in 1271 (or according to some sources, 1275), Jnaneshwar Maharaj, as he is honorifically called, ushered in a revolutionary movement of *bhakti,* devotion, which shunned ritual and formalism in favor of an intensely personal relationship to the divine, establishing love of the divine as a direct path to the highest spiritual state. He showed, through his life, that *moksha,* liberation, was not the property of the elite and the prosperous who recited Sanskrit mantras and convened great *yagnas,* fire sacrifices, but was open to one and all; the only entrance fee being the yearning for God.

At the age of nineteen, Jnaneshwar wrote one of the most authoritative, beautiful, and unique commentaries in a *prakrit* (people's) language on the *Bhagavad Gita*. The *Bhagavad Gita* is a key Indian philosophical text of about 700 verses, and his commentary, called *Jnaneshwari,* has over 9000 verses. Jnaneshwar, or *Jnandev,* as he is also known, also wrote some 1000 poems, not generally available in English, as well as two dense philosophical works, *Amritanubhava, The Nectar of Awareness;* and *Changdev Pasashti, Sixty-Five Stanzas for Changdev.* An excellent prose rendering of the *Jnaneshwari* and a poetic translation of *Amritanubhava* are available in English.[1] However, his 1000 poems, or *abhangas,* remain largely unavailable. This book is an effort to bring a sampling of them to the modern English-speaking audience.

JNANESHWAR'S LIFE

Jnaneshwar's poetry is gentle. It is hard to find a harsh phrase anywhere in his vast corpus. Yet Jnaneshwar's life was a stark contrast to the joy he has brought to millions. He and his entire family suffered cruelties and deprivations all their life. Living in a time of inhuman and brutal religious fanaticism, the family was not accepted by the established hierarchy, and was persecuted ruthlessly. Jnaneshwar's father, Vitthalapant, was forced to commit suicide because he had returned to householder life after having taken monk's vows. Vitthalapant's children—Jnaneshwar and three siblings—were ostracized, shunned, and persecuted. They couldn't even buy basic necessities such as a stove; no one would sell any goods to them. Often there was nothing to eat. An image cherished by the Marathi people depicts Muktabai, Jnaneshwar's younger sister, roasting *chapatis,* or bread, on Jnaneshwar's back, which he had "heated up" like a stove through his yogic powers.

Jnaneshwar's older brother by three years was Nivritti, his Guru and preceptor. Nivritti, it is said, had been instructed in a cave, into which he had run while escaping from a tiger. There, the tradition goes, Gahininath, a sage in the non-dual Shaivite Nath lineage, gave Nivritti the knowledge of the supreme truth in seven straight days. Nivritti in turn instructed Jnaneshwar and the other two siblings, Sopan and Muktabai, who also attained that same knowledge. As the Indian tradition would explain it, they thus became liberated, freed from the inevitable wheel of human suffering, and lived in such a liberated state the rest of their lives.

Quite a family. They all wrote poems. However, it was Jnaneshwar who was the most prolific; his corpus, a veritable ocean, contains a total count of well over 10,000 verses. In fact, approaching Jnaneshwar is a bit like approaching the ocean. Getting near his words calms one's being. We can bathe in them and let the eternal rhythm of his verses wash over us. The verses keep swelling with lofty emotions, rolling out of some unknown depth, cleansing the mind again and again in ever fresh images, no two ever the same yet all filled with that magical haunting sound of the deep.

Jnaneshwar's dying was just as extraordinary as his life. At the age of twenty-two, having completed his major pieces of work, Jnaneshwar asked his Guru and brother, Nivritti, for permission to "retire." When Nivritti finally agreed, Jnaneshwar entered a state of *samadhi*, complete union with the divine, stepping into a small enclosure that received him alive.

Three hundred years later, the great Marathi poet-saint Eknath, upon receiving instruction from Jnaneshwar in a dream, opened up the samadhi shrine to remove a piece of root from the peepul tree that was strangling

Jnaneshwar's throat. To the Marathi heart, Jnaneshwar is still as good as alive. To this day, there is an unending line of pilgrims gathered at his samadhi shrine in Alandi, to read his words, feel his palpable presence, and receive his blessings.

JNANESHWAR, A SPIRITUAL REVOLUTIONARY

Most of Jnaneshwar's compositions are loosely bound in the *ovi* meter, which consists of four lines, the first three with eight syllables, and the last line with four syllables. Ovi literally means "strung"—a meter on which inner truths would be strung.

Jnaneshwar's ovi works became the foundation of the rich tradition of the Marathi poet saints. The *Varkari* poets, as they were sometimes called, included Jnaneshwar's contemporaries, such as Namdev, Visoba Khechar, and Janabai; as well as Eknath and Tukaram, who lived centuries later. Coming from the common stock, they were all engaged in modest livelihoods. For example, Sena was a barber, Gora was a potter, and Tukaram was an oil merchant. But they all had one thing in common: their uncompromising love of the divine and their attainment of the supreme goal of life, which, according to the Hindu mystical tradition, is oneness with the truth. They all, without exception, acknowledged their debt to Jnaneshwar and followed his way of melding knowledge and love in a seamless flow, making it impossible for the heart not to reach out to the supreme nor for the supreme to resist such a heart.

In essence, Jnaneshwar simply espoused union with the divine. Yet the knowledge and experience of God that Jnaneshwar facilitated was so immediate and strong that he ended up facilitating a revolution. The thirteenth century was a dark age in central India. The entrenchment of the Brahmin establishment had rendered the ancient traditions increasingly stale and lifeless. The caste system facilitated a power hierarchy where material, political, and spiritual knowledge were subsumed by the elite few. In this environment, Jnaneshwar ushered in the era of the ecstatic *Varkari Sampradaya,* the traditional cymbal-clanging, God-loving, God-seeking culture that returned God to where he belonged: the hearts of the people.

Even today, hundreds of thousands of people annually congregate in the Marathi-speaking region of Maharashtra, starting, among other places, from Jnaneshwar's home. There, gathering momentum, traveling from village to village, they dance and sing *Vitthal, Vitthal,* in on-going cascades of joy, finally pouring into the village of Pandharpur, the home of their beloved deity Vitthal (whose picture is on the cover of this book). To this day, the *waari,* as this annual pilgrimage is called, opens with the first poem of Jnaneshwar's collection, the *Gaathaa*:

Roopa paahataa lochani
Sukha tzaale wo saajanee
To haa Vitthala baravaa
To haa maadhava baravaa

To lay your eyes on Him
is happiness, O beloved.
That Vitthal, that Madhav
is the one I seek.

It's the merit of countless good deeds
that I love Him,
that storehouse of bliss,
Lord of the great goddess.

POWER OF HIS WORDS

The riches of the Marathi language are impressive. Spoken in the central-western region of India, Maharashtra, it has nurtured an abundance of prose and poetry. However, in the words of R. D. Ranade, "There hasn't been, nor will there ever be, another (like Jnaneshwar)."[2]

His mastery over the language and the meter was so supreme that reading his poetry is more like listening to music. Another scholar W.B. Patwardhan wrote, "It is an instrument that he has only to touch and it responds…Unparalleled in Marathi literature, *Jnaneshwari* is so exquisite, so beautiful, so poetic in its metaphors, its similes, its analogies, so lofty in its style, so sublime in its tone, so melodious, so original in its concepts, so pure in taste ......that the reader is simply fascinated, floats rapturously on the crest of its flow, is lost in the cadence of its rhythm and its sweet harmonies, till all is thanksgiving and thought is not."[3]

Uncharacteristically, for Jnaneshwar was the very image of humility, he himself says in *Jnaneshwari,*

My Marathi speech, simple,
will win over nectar itself,
such words shall I form
with feeling.[4]

Jnaneshwar's poetry engages one's entire being; one may read or hear his words, yet it is more as if one tastes them, such is their sweetness. Every word, every phrase has but one purpose and one effect: to pull the reader to his innermost core, and drench him in his own inner power, his own inner love.

Perhaps Jnaneshwar's words have such power because he had found his way to the source of life and joy, a source he experienced as the Self, or core, of all. He talks ceaselessly of his awareness that all beings are, at heart, one. Is it any wonder then that he could reach so many with his speech and his call? His call was the call of love and his vision, a vision of equality. Strikingly modern in his uncompromising vision of equality, and thoroughly ancient in his reach of love, the nurturing in his poetry is felt immediately. Speak to anybody in Pune, a modern Indian city now a bustling hub of IT, and they will talk of Jnaneshwar as *Jnaneshwar Maooli,* "Jnaneshwar, the mother," using this most intimate term *maooli,* which is the equivalent of *mamma.*

His *ovis* are sung to children as lullabies, as in, for example, the following:

Hari aala re Hari aala re
Santa sange brahmaananda tsaalaa re

Hari has come, Hari has come.
With the saints the joy of Brahman has come.

Jnaneshwar points out that Hari, the beloved and familiar Lord Krishna, is the same as Brahman, the formless absolute. Imagine—because of the beauty of his song, Jnaneshwar's influence starts in the cradle, as young babies nurse on the highest philosophy, sweetened and made easily digestible by Jnaneshwar's melodic words.

THE MANY FACETS OF JNANESHWAR

Approaching Jnaneshwar is like approaching a gem of a thousand facets. Depending upon where you stand, it reveals a different shade, a different color. Jnaneshwar the disciple had unparalleled humility. Despite his powerful influence on everyone, Jnaneshwar simply credited his

Guru Nivritti with all of his power. In Chapter 18 of *Jnaneshwari*, we read:

What is it that is not possible by the Guru's grace,
by whose grace the moon cools,
and the earth never tires of its creatures,
by whose power the wind blows
and the sky is spacious?
That supremely compassionate Guru
has taken up residence in me
and operates through me.
What wonder then that even my breath,
ever new, ever fresh,
becomes poetry?

Sometimes Jnaneshwar may seem like a man of knowledge, erudite, the master himself. And this indeed he was, true to his name. One anecdote relays his interaction with Changdev, a great and accomplished yogi who, despite his miraculous attainments, had still not found rest. Tradition goes that he came to meet Jnaneshwar riding a tiger and holding a snake for a whip. Jnaneshwar and his siblings were sitting on a ledge. In order to "receive" him, Jnaneshwar asked the ledge to fly. And the ledge did. In *Changdev Pasashti,* or *Sixty-Five Stanzas for Changdev,* Jnaneshwar speaks to the proud yogi about *kaivalya,* the state of that-in-itself, one-alone, pure consciousness, completely free, completely independent of bodily identification:

That One, who exists when nothing else is,
that One who is seen when nothing else is,
that One who is enjoyed when nothing else is,
that One Alone.

Then there is Jnaneshwar, the consummate yogi, the master of his body, senses, and life force, able to channel the subtle life energy through ever subtler stages of being. For example, in poem numbered 807, Jnaneshwar offers a complete map of the path of the inner spiritual energy, the *Kundalini,* through the various *chakras,* centers of consciousness in the body, the celebrated chakras that yogis work at piercing in their quest to reach the *sahasrar,* the abode of the infinite. His description perfectly matches the path of spiritual awakening described in yogic and tantric texts.

At other times, Jnaneshwar looks like a devotee, a mad lover of God, who cares for nothing but to feast his eyes on the form of his beloved Vitthal, the Lord of Pandharpur. Pandharpur, a village a few miles from the city of Pune, hosts the *murti,* or statue, of Vitthal, a unique form of Krishna standing akimbo with his hands on his waist, just waiting, they say, for his devotees.

Beholding with no-mind
his dark grandeur parades, delights, reigns supreme.
This form, priceless, this fine, fine form.
Therefore I say with a pure heart,
Lord of the great Goddess Rukmini,
fathomless, dark,
everything, everywhere has become an offering.

PHILOSOPHY IN JNANESHWAR'S WORKS

In *Jnaneshwari,* Jnaneshwar speaks of his lineage as coming from Shiva, the great original Lord, *Adi Nath,* through Matsyendranath, Gorakhnath, Gahininath, to his brother Nivrittinath. This lineage of non-dual Shaivites believed in and lived the experience of the unity of all creation with the supreme God-head, the one-without-a-second. This unity beyond all description is named *Shiva*. Hence the word *Shaivite*.

The Naths were also masters of *shaktipat*, the awakening of the Kundalini energy. *Shaktipat* literally means the "descent of grace." The universal energy, depicted in Shaivite scriptures as a maiden, creates the universe out of Herself, maintains it as Herself, and re-absorbs the universe into Herself. She also hides from Herself, becoming the individual self who feels cut off from the supreme source of life. And She reveals Herself to the individual in an act of grace. This act of revelation is shaktipat.

In one verse, for example, Jnaneshwar references Kundalini as the youthful maiden:

Youthful maiden dwelling in the sky,
all three worlds in her belly
united with the sound,
supreme witness at the door of creation.

The "sky" is the space of awareness, *chidakash*. The "door of creation" refers to the *brahma-randhra*, the opening of Brahman. The paradoxical descriptions in this verse are typical of Jnaneshwar: the youthful maiden, ever young, is pregnant with the three worlds. She is one with the supreme sound, *paravak*, the first throb of creation, yet she is the witness.

Jnaneshwar is fully at home with the philosophy of Kashmir Shaivism, or more accurately *Trika Shastra*, the non-dual school that flourished in Kashmir, India, preceding the time of Jnaneshwar. A detailed one-to-one mapping can be made between trika and Jnaneshwar's philosophy, found primarily in *Amritanubhav*, and in some of his poems. For example, this first verse from *Changdev Pasashti:*

We praise the Lord
upon whose hiding, the world is seen
and upon whose revealing himself, the world disappears.

The verse reminds us of the first verse of a foundational Kashmir Shaivite text, *Spanda Karikas*, which says, "We laud that Lord, upon whose opening his eyes, the world manifests, and upon whose closing them, the world disappears."[5]

Jnaneshwar is also comfortable with the yogic philosophies, such as when he expounds *Ashtanga Yoga* in the sixth chapter in *Jnaneshwari*. And perhaps even Buddhists may find his words intriguing, with his numerous references to the void or various types of voids leading to the supreme void and beyond, as in poem 815:

Here are the four voids
and the great void beyond.
The color of the Self
drenches them all.

Or in poem 102:

Rest, rest, beloved, rest,
rest like a baby
in the cradle of the formless.
Being the void
rest in the void.

BEYOND ALL WORDS AND PHILOSOPHY

Above all, Jnaneshwar was a knower of the truth, and was at all times ecstatically merged with it. Knowing that the truth was beyond the pale of words, and driven both by a compulsion to share his experience and to awaken others to it, he unstintingly used whatever words and forms he needed to awaken the reader to this state. His writings are full of a peculiar use of paradoxical images, whose beauty and harmonic sounds conceal the inner effect of those paradoxes: to catapult the reader's consciousness beyond the mind into that which is the source of the mind:

Words don't reach there, debates are silenced;
one principle, without form, without duality,
that one from Pandharpur, exquisite of form,
storehouse of blue
fills all, the moving and the unmoving.
My own, reflected in my house,
Lord of the great goddess.

The contrasts and paradoxes in this poem, typical for Jnaneshwar, are both sublime and philosophically profound. The verse juxtaposes and unifies opposites: "without form" with "exquisite of form," "moving" with "unmoving." "Storehouse of blue" hints at the yogic experience of the ultimate. Finally, Jnaneshwar merges the transcendent and the immanent, the Lord and the devotee, by calling upon a Shaivite concept, *bimba* and *pratibimba,* meaning the original and the reflection. Brahman, the absolute, is *bimba.* His reflection, *pratibimba,* is the individual self.

But then Jnaneshwar adds his unique tapestry to it: I am His reflection, He is the real one, yet He belongs to me! This "belonging" is the belonging in love, in *paraa-bhakti.*

What appears patently contradictory is reconciled in a higher truth, as we see this Shaivite master established in the formless, singing hymns of love and devotion to the form of Vitthal. We are not surprised when ultimately, Jnaneshwar says that love is the way and love is the destination.

We hope you enjoy Jnaneshwar's songs of love to the Divine, the Self of all, the ancient, the primordial One.

Source for the verses:

SSG Joshi, Kashinath Ananta, ed., *Sakala Sant Gaathaa*.

NOTES

1. See the bibliography for sources containing these translations.
2. R.D. Ranade in *Jnaneshwar Vachanamrita,* quoted in *Sartha Jnaneshwari* by S.V. and Mamasaheb Dandekar, Poona, 1973.
3. W.B. Patwardhan, *Wilson Philological Lectures,* lecture 3, quoted in *Sartha Jnaneshwari* by S.V. and Mamasaheb Dandekar, Poona, 1973.
4. *Jnaneshwari,* VI-14.
5. See, e.g., Jaideva Singh, *Spanda Karikas.*

ABHANGAS

रूप पाहतां लोचनीं
सुख जालें वो साजणी

तो हा विठ्ठल बरवा
तो हा माधव बरवा

बहुता सुकृतांची जोडी
म्हणुनि विठ्ठलीं आवडी

सर्व सुखाचें आगरु
बापरखुमादेवीवरु

(SSG 1)

To lay your eyes on Him
is happiness, O beloved.
That Vitthal, that Madhav
is the one I seek.[1]

It's the merit of countless good deeds
that I love Him,
that storehouse of bliss,
Lord of the great goddess.[2]

(SSG 1)

चिदानंद रूप चेतवितें एक
एकपणें गुणागुणीं दावी अनेक

आदि अंतीं गुण सर्वत्र निर्गुण
गुणासी अगुण भासतीना

कैसें जालें अरुपीं गुणीं गुणवृत्ती
सगुण पाहतां अंतरलें गती

बापरखुमादेविरु विठ्ठलु नंदनंदनु
आदिअंतु एकु पूर्ण सनातनु गे माये

(SSG 2)

That mass of conscious bliss,
putting His oneness on fire,
shows in His oneness
the many.[3]

These forms
from beginning to end
are all the formless;
but form does not see
the un-form.[4]

How come this—
these qualities, ever-changing,
ever forming,
ever springing from the formless?

See His form;
lose wandering,
lose becoming.

Lord of the great goddess,
Vitthal, joy of Nanda,[5]
from beginning to end
always the One;
the perfect,
the ancient,
the primordial.

(SSG 2)

मन मुरडोनि डोळां लेइलें
काळेपणें मिरविलें रूप त्याचें

बरवें रूप काळें अमोलिक
म्हणोनियां सांगतसे शुद्ध भावें

रखुमादेवीवरु अगाध काळें
म्हणोनि सर्वत्र अर्पियेलें

(SSG 3)

Turned my mind,
came to see
his deep darkness[6]
dancing.

This lovely form,
dark and priceless,
hence I speak
in pure-speak.

Lord of the great goddess,
dark, fathomless,
everything has become
an offering.[7]

(SSG 3)

हरपली सत्ता मुराली वासना
सांवळाचि नयना दिसतसे

काय करूं माय सांवळा श्रीकृष्ण
सांगितला प्रश्न निवृत्तीनें

बापरखुमादेविवरु सांवळीये तेज
सेजबाज निज कृष्ण सुखें

(SSG 4)

Lost is the grip
of being and pulling.
All we see
is the dark one.

There is no doing now,
just his dark, dark form.
Nivritti has shown us
the secret.[8]

Lord of the great goddess,
blinding dark light,
everything is soaked in bliss.[9]

(SSG 4)

नवल देखिलें कृष्णरूपीं बिंब
सांवळी स्वयंभ मूर्ति हरिची

मन निवालें बिंबलें समाधान जालें
कृष्णरूपें बोधलें मन माझें

बापरखुमादेविवरु सांवळा सर्व घटीं
चित्तें चैतन्या मिठी घालिताखेवों

(SSG 5)

What a wondrous sight,
image of Krishna,
this dark form of Hari
unborn, revealed.[10]

My mind has ceased moving,
has imbibed Him, satisfied.
This dark form has instructed me
into the mystery.

Lord of the great goddess,
dark one in every vessel,
my mind has embraced
the conscious.[11]

(SSG 5)

मूळ ना डाळ शाखा ना पल्लव
तो हा कैसा देव आलां घरीं

निर्गुणपणें उभा सगुणपणें शोभा
जिवाशिवा प्रभा दाविताहे

नकळे याची गती नकळे याची लीळा
आपिआप सोहळा भोगीतसे

ज्ञानदेव म्हणे न कळे याची थोरी
आपण चराचरीं नांदतसे

(SSG 7)

He has arrived
no root, no trunk; no branch, no leaf.
He has arrived
rooted in the formless
illuminating all [12]
with his form.

None can know his play,
none can know his way.
He is the enjoyer;
He is the all.

Jnandev says,
unfathomable is his glory.
He sports within all
moving and the unmoving.

(SSG 7)

कांहीं नव्हे तो
अमूर्ता मूर्ति तो गे बाई

सहजा सहज तो
सहज सुखनिधान तो गे बाई

बापरखुमादेविवरु तो
पुंडलिकवरद तो गे बाई

(SSG 16)

He is naught, naught is He;
form of the formless,
formless is He.

Nature of the natural [13]
abode of natural joy, He.
Lord of the great goddess
giver of boons to the devotee,[14] He.

(SSG 16)

निज ब्रह्मा ब्रह्म तो
ब्रह्मादिकां वंद्य तो गे बाई

अचिंतचिंतन तो
सारासार गुह्य तो गे बाई

बापरखुमादेविवरु विठ्ठलु तो
जनीं वनीं कृपाळु तो गे बाई

(SSG 17)

The inner essence of creation,
honored by all.[15]
Beyond contemplation,
beyond thought.

Pure mystery,
object of contemplation,
the essence
and the conclusion of all.

Lord of the great goddess
benevolent, compassionate
whether in solitude
or not.

(SSG 17)

पैल गोल्हाटमंडळ तो
त्रिकुटा वेगळा तो गे बाई

सहजबोधीं अनुभव तो
परमतत्वीं अनुराग तो गे बाई

रखुमादेविवरु तो
ब्रह्म विटेवरी तो गे बाई

(SSG 20)

Beyond the twists and turns of practice, He.
Past the exalted states of yoga, He.[16]

Seen naturally, directly, He.
Love of the supreme, He.[17]

Lord of the great goddess, He.
Standing on the brick, image of the Absolute, He.[18]

(SSG 20)

सांवळेचें तेज सांवळें बिंबलें
प्रेम तें घातलें हृदयघटीं

निरालंब बाज निरालंब तेज
चित्तरस निज निजतेजें

आदिमध्यअंत राहिला अनंत
न दिसे द्वैताद्वैत आम्हां रया[19]

ज्ञानदेवीं सोय अवघाचि सामाय
सुखदुःख माय आम्हां नाहीं

(SSG 25)

Blinding dark light
funneling into that dark form,
pouring love into the vessel of the heart;
sound and light leaning on nothing,
the essence of the mind [20]
with its brilliance.

Nectar of the Self
in the beginning, middle, and the end;
none left but the boundless one.
We see neither separation nor its absence.

Jnandev says,
He fills us in his fullness.[21]
We know neither pleasure nor pain.

(SSG 25)

आकारेंवीण पाळणा पहुडलें
निराकार म्हणोनि वोसणाईलें

जो जो जो जो बाळा निराकार पाळणा
व्योमीं व्योमाकारीं झोंप घेई

चौदा नि:शब्दीं जागृत केलें
येकवीसीं हालवूनि बाळ उठविलें

बापरखुमादेविवरु निजीं निजविलें
कांहीं नव्हे ऐसें कांहीं ना केलें

(SSG 102)

Having shed form, he rests.
Formless, he coos in his sleep.

Rest, rest, beloved, rest,
rest like a baby
in the cradle of the formless;
being the void,
rest in the void.

Without uttering a word,
He woke me up into the wordless,
shaking up my universe.[22]

Lord of the great goddess
has me resting in Himself,[23]
made me as nothing
doing nothing.

(SSG 102)

इवलेंसें रोप लाविलें द्वारीं
त्याचा वेल गेला गगनावरी

मोगरा फुलला मोगरा फुलला
फुलें वेंचिता अतिभारु कळियांसि आला

मनाचिये गुंती गुंफियेला शेला
बापरखुमादेविवर विठ्ठलीं अर्पिला

(SSG 234)

Tiny seedling planted at the door
grew into a vine straddling the sky.

It's blooming, it's flowering,
picking a few brings out a flood of more.

Garland woven from the knots of the mind
offered to Vitthal, Lord of the great goddess.[24]

(SSG 234)

अंतरींच्या सुखा नाहीं पै मर्यादा
यापरी अगाधा होउनी खोल

तेथें गोविंदु अवघाचि जाला
विश्व व्यापुनिया उरला असे

बाह्य अभ्यंतरीं नाहीं आपपार
सर्व निरंतर नारायण

मीपण माझें न देखे दुजें
ज्ञानदेवो म्हणे ऐसे केलें निवृत्तिराजें

(SSG 238)

There is no limit to the joy inside,
limitless, deep, profound.

Deep down there, Govinda has become all,
pervading the universe, and then some more.[25]

Inside, outside, there is no limit to Him.
All is Narayana, forever Narayana.

My I-ness can't register another.
This is what my Lord Nivritti has done.

(SSG 238)

लेउनि अंजन दाविलें निधान
देखतांचि मन मावळलें

ऐसिया सुखाचे करूनियां आळें
बीज तें निर्मळ पेरी आतां

ज्ञानाचा हा वाफा भरूनियां कमळीं
सतरावी निराळी तिंबतसे

निवृत्ति प्रसादें पावलों या सुखा
उजळलीया रेखा ज्ञानाचिया

(SSG 239)

Applying the lotion,
he showed me the bounty
and the mind dissolved.

Having prepared the soil of joy,
he sowed the immaculate seed
overflowing the heart [26]
with knowing.

Now everything is soaked
in the supreme.[27]

Something marvelous has happened.
Nivritti's grace has brought joy.
The flower of knowledge has bloomed.[28]

(SSG 239)

मी माझें द्वैत अद्वैत होउनि ठेलें
सद्‌गुरु एका बोलें ठेविलें ठायीं

द्वैत गिळी अद्वैत मेळीं
चित्ताची काजळी तोडी वेगीं

ज्ञानदेव म्हणे निवृत्ति उदार
दीपीं दीप स्थिर केला सोयी

(SSG 240)

Transforming the dualities of me and mine
into non-duality,
transporting me to the station
with but one word of the master.

Swallowing duality, bestowing the non-dual,
the darkness of the mind is broken.

Says Jnandev, he is generous, that Nivritti.
He steadied the flame into the Flame.
Easily.

(SSG 240)

अरे अरे ज्ञाना झालासि पावन
तुझें तुज ध्यान कळों आलें

तुझा तूंचि देव तुझा तूंचि भाव
फिटला संदेह अन्यतत्वीं

मुरडूनियां मन उपजलासि चित्तें
कोठें तुज रितें न दिसे रया

दीपकीं दीपक मावळल्या ज्योती
घरभरी वाती शून्य झाल्या

वृत्तीची निवृत्ति आपणासकट
अवघेंची वैकुंठ चतुर्भुज

निवृत्ति परमाअनुभव नेमा
शांति पूर्ण क्षमा ज्ञानदेवो

(SSG 245)

Oh, what good fortune, Jnana,[29]
you have been made holy,
you have realized what it means to meditate on
yourself.

You are your own Lord, your own feeling,[30]
all doubt about that one-without-a-second is gone.

Having bent the mind, he made it such
it can't see anything empty
of Him.

Flames have merged into the Flame,
every wick in the house is empty.

The mind has been unburdened of its fickle, along
with the self;[31]
all, everything, is heaven, the Lord.

Nivritti, forgiving all, gave Jnandev the
unmistakable
supreme experience, perfect peace.[32]

(SSG 245)

परेसी जंव पाहे तंव दिसे हें अरुतें
तळीं तळाखालतें विश्वरूप

दिव्य चक्षुदृष्टि निवृत्तीनें दिधली
अवघीच बुझाली विष्णुमाया

शम दम कळा दांत उदांत
शांतितत्व मावळत उपरमेसी

गगनीं दिनमणि गगनासकट[33]
अवघेचि वैकुंठ तया घरीं

उद्‌भट कारण केलें हो ऐसें
तुष्टोनि सौरसें केलें तुम्ही

ज्ञानदेव शरण निवृत्तीच्या चरणा
कांसवीचा पान्हा पाजियेला

(SSG 246)

Look beyond[34] that you may see what's at hand;
go deep within, see His form as the universe.

Nivritti gave us the divine vision.
Now the whole play is over

The doings, undoings, the prescribed, the proscribed,
the sun along with the sky,
all peacefully dissolve in the end,
turning everything at home into heaven.

You have done something wonderful,
pleased with me, you have blessed me sweetly.

Jnandev takes refuge at Nivritti's feet,
drinking the nectar beyond all imagining.

(SSG 246)

ऐसें हे अंडज सांगितलें देवें
सांगोनिया भावें गिळीयेलें

गिळिला प्रपंच समाप्ति इंद्रियां
वैष्णवी हे माया बिंबाकार

निरशून्य शून्य साधूनि उपरम
वैकुंठीचें धाम हृदय केलें

जिव शिव शेजे पंक्तीस बैसली
पंचतत्वांची बोली नाहीं तेथें

तत्वीं तत्व गेलें बोलणें वैखरी
वेदवक्ते चारी मान्य झाले

ज्ञानदेव म्हणे निवृत्ति तुष्टला
सर्वांगें दिधला समबोध

(SSG 247)

He taught me the secret of creation.
I proceeded to swallow that which was born, with
the tool of *bhavana.*[35]

I swallowed relationships, senses, the entire creation;
came to see that manifestation is the same as the
source.[36]

By mastering the void and the no-void, stopping,[37]
I made my heart the abode of heaven.

The individual and the supreme now sit side by side,
feasting.[38]
What then of the elements?

The principle merged into the Principle.
The tongue tries to speak.
The Vedas agree.

Jnandev says, Nivritti was pleased
and drowned my body in equality.[39]

(SSG 247)

सत्व रज तम प्रकृती अपारा
याहि भिन्न प्रकारा हरि रया

दिसोनि न दिसे लोकीं व्यापारी
घटमठ चाह्ली हरि व्याप्त

स्वानुभवें धरी अनुभवें वाट
तंव अवचित बोभाट पुढे मागें

ज्ञानदेव म्हणे न कळे याची लीला
ते निवृत्तीनें डोळां दाविली मज

(SSG 248)

Light, movement, and inertia,
clarity, restlessness, indolence,[40]
all are manifestations of His ways.

Hidden in the obvious,
in the comings and goings,
He pervades all.[41]

Hold Him with your experience.
Each thing screams his name[42]
unexpectedly.

Jnandev says, Nivritti has shown me[43]
that which cannot be seen,
His unfathomable play.

(SSG 248)

तृप्ति भुकेली काय करूं माये
जीवनीं जीवन कैसें तान्हेजत आहे

मन धालें परि न धाये
पुढत पुढती राजा विठ्ठलु पाहे

निरंजनीं अंजन लेइजत आहे
आपुलें निधान कैसें आपणची पाहे

निवृत्ति गार्हस्थ्य मांडलें आहे
निष्काम आपत्य प्रसवत जाये

त्रिभुवनीं आनंदु न मायेगे माये
आपेआपु परमानंदु वोसंडतु आहे

बापरखुमादेविवरू विठ्ठलुगे माये
देहंभाव सांडूनि भोगिजत आहे

(SSG 250)

Satisfaction is famished, life is thirsting for life;
the mind, though satiated, is ever so thirsty
for the King.

The one who is beyond seeing
is all eyes for his own glory.

Nivritti has taken up householdership
breeding desirelessness.[44]

Three worlds can't contain this bliss supreme
overflowing on its own.

My Father, Lord of the great goddess,
enjoys,[45]
giving up body consciousness.

(SSG 250)

अमित्य भुवनीं भरलें शेखीं जें उरलें
तें रूप आपुले मज दावियलें वो माये

आतां मी नये आपुलिया आस
सुटले सायास भ्रांतीचे वो माये

मंजुळ मंजुळ वायो गती झळकती
तापत्रयें निवृत्ति निर्वाळिलें वो माय

वेडावलें एकाएकी निजधाम रूपीं
रखुमादेविवरु दीपीं दिव्य तेज वो माय

(SSG 266)

The one who remains after filling the universe,
that immeasurable one showed Himself to me.

Now I don't fret over myself;
why, the net of misapprehension has been broken.

A gentle breeze blows,
cooling the terrible fires.[46]

Unexpectedly He made me his own,
made me go mad for his form, his station,
Lord of the great goddess, supreme light of the light.

(SSG 266)

शुद्धमतीगती मज वोळला निवृत्ती
त्याने पदीं पदीं प्रीति स्वरूपीं वो माय

आतां मी जाईन आपुलिया गांवा
होईल विसावा सुखसागरीं वो माय

पाहातां न देखे आपुलें कोणी नाहीं
निजरूप पाही अनंता नयनीं वो माय

हा रखुमादेविवरु गुरुगम्य सागरु
न करीच अव्हेरु माझा वो माय

(SSG 267)

Nivritti showed me the pure vision,
now it's love at every step.

I am on my way home now,
finally resting
in an ocean of joy.

Find as I may, I can't find any not mine.
I see my own Self, infinitely, everywhere.

Lord of the great goddess, this ocean, Guru's gift,[47]
He does not neglect me.

(SSG 267)

मजमाज पाहतां मीपण हरपलें
ठकलेंचि ठेलें सये मन माझें

आंत विठ्ठल बाहेर विठ्ठल
मीचि विठ्ठल मज भासतसे

मीपण माझे नुरेचि कांहीं दुजें
ऐसें केलें निवृत्तिराजें म्हणे ज्ञानदेवो

(SSG 277)

I looked within myself
and I lost my *me*,
my mind
came to a complete halt.

Inside, Vitthal; outside, Vitthal;
me myself am Vitthal.

This is how it is now.
Everything has become my me-ness;
  there is no other left.[48]
This is what he did, that King Nivritti, says Jnandev.
This is what that great king of the gurus did.[49]

(SSG 277)

निजाचें तेज कीं तेजाचे निज
तेथील तें गुज सांग मज

ब्रह्म तें कायी ब्रह्म तें कायी
ब्रह्म तें कायी सांगा गोसावी

ब्रह्म सदोदित असे सर्वभूतीं
म्हणौनि सांगे जनाप्रती

ब्रह्म ऐसे नामयाने जाणितलें
हृदयीं धरिलें प्राणलिंग

बापरखुमादेविवरु हृदयीं प्रगटला
निवांत राहिला ज्ञानदेवो

(SSG 287)

Effulgence of the Self
or the Self of the effulgence?
Tell me the secret, bring it home to me.

What is this Brahman,
what Brahman is this?
Brahman the absolute is forever risen in beings.
Hence I keep telling, everybody.

Namdev understood this Brahman,
held him in his heart as his very life.[50]

Lord of the great goddess
is revealed in my heart.
Jnandev sits now,
still.

(SSG 287)

आकारीं नाहीं तें निराकारीं पाही
निराकारीं राही शून्याशून्य

जेथें शून्यचि मावळलें तेथें काय उरलें
हेचि सांगे एके बोलें मजपासीं

शून्य कासया पासाव जाले शून्य तें कवणें केलें
हें सांगिजोजि एक्या बोलें गुरुराया

आपण शून्याकार कीं आपण निराकार
आकार निराकार मूर्तिमंत दाऊं

आकार निराकार ये दोन्ही नाहीं
तेंचि तूं पाही आपणापें

जेथे अनुभवचि नाहीं तेंचि तूं पाही
स्वानुभवीं राही तुझा तूंचि

जेथे चंद्र सूर्य एक होती तेथें कैचि दिनराती
ऐसे जे जाणती ते योगेश्वर

कर्माकर्म पारुषलें देवधर्म लोपले
गुरुशिष्या निमाले जाले क्षीरसिंधु

तेथें गोडीवीण चाखणें जिव्हेवीण बोलणें
नेत्रेंवीण पाहणें तेंचि ब्रह्म

हातीं घेऊनियां दिवटी लागिजे अंधारापाठीं
अंधार न देखे दृष्टी उजियेडु तो

बापरखुमादेविवरु विठ्ठलु देखणा
दृष्यद्रष्टेपणा माल्हावले

(SSG 288)

The one whom form cannot hold,
see Him in the formless;
He dwells there as the void of the void.

When the void itself disappears,
what then is left?
What void is this; where does it come from?
Let's show you, said the King.

Which one are you, form of the void or formless? [51]
Neither form nor formless,
this is what you have to see
on your own.

That seeing you must see
where there is no seeing
on your own,
abiding in yourself, by yourself.[52]

When the sun and the moon become one,[53]
whither night, whither day?
Knowing this is to know;
such a one has done something.[54]
There, good action, bad action, right action,
wrong action,
seeker, preceptor, all dissolve into the ocean of
consciousness.

Tasting without taste-buds,
speaking without tongue,
seeing without eyes,
that one is Brahman.

Taking a lamp in the hand,
you go out chasing darkness,
can't find it anywhere
because your eyes are filled with light.

He is something to see,
father, Lord of the great goddess.
This whole business of the seer and the seen is gone.

(SSG 288)

देहाचेनि दीपकें पाहे जों सभोंवतें
तंव अवचितेंची ध्यान केलें

निराकारींची वस्तु आकारा आणिली
कृष्णीं कृष्ण केली सकळ सृष्टी

लय गेले ध्यानीं ध्यान गेले उन्मनी
नित्य हरिपर्वणी सर्वांरूपें

आनंद सोहळा हरिरूपीं आवडी
कृष्ण अर्धघडी न सोडी आम्हां

बापरखुमादेविवरविठ्ठल अभय
भयांचें पैं भय हरपे कृष्णीं

(SSG 290)

One who looks around with the lamp of the body,
all of a sudden, turns everything into meditation.

Turning formless substance into form,[55]
Krishna has turned it all into himself.

Absorption turned into meditation, meditation into
unmani, no-mind;
there is only a festival of Hari now in every form.[56]

What a feast, what a joy,
this affection for the form of Hari.
He does not leave us now, not for a second.

Vitthal, my father, fearless,
Lord of the great goddess,
fear after fear disappear into Him.

(SSG 290)

सकळ तीर्थें निवृत्तीच्या पायीं
तेथें बुडी देई माझ्या मना

आतां मी न करी चित्ताचें भ्रमण
वृत्तीसी मार्जन केलें असे

एकार्णव जाला तरंगु बुडाला
तैसा देह जाला एकरूप

बापरखुमादेविवीवरें विठ्ठलें नवल पैं केलें
तारूं हरविलें मृगजळीं

(SSG 291)

All holy rivers are at the feet of Nivritti;[57]
that's where I take my mind bathing.

There is no more wandering for me;
the tendencies are cleansed forever.

Like a wave drowning into the ocean
my body has become One.[58]

What a miracle He has done.
Lord of the great goddess, my father Vitthal,
took my boat across the mirage.

(SSG 291)

अवघाची संसार सुखाचा करीन
आनंदें भरीन तिन्ही लोक

जाईनगे माये तया पंढरपुरा
भेटेन माहेरा आपुलिया

सर्व सुकृताचे फळ मी लाहीन
क्षेम मी देईन परब्रह्मीं

बापरखुमादेविवरा विठ्ठलाची भेटी
आपुलिये संवसाटी घेउनि राहे

(SSG 295)

I shall fill the whole world with joy,
I shall make this entire world happy,[59]

I shall go to the Lord's dwelling,
I shall go home.[60]

I will enjoy the fruits of my good actions,
I shall be fulfilled in the absolute.[61]

My father, the Lord of the great goddess,
one meeting with Him
and He makes you his own.

(SSG 295)

विठ्लयात्रे जाति वो माये
त्याचे धरीन मी पायें

विठोबा माझें माहेर
भेटेन बुद्धि परिकर

रखुमादेविवर विठ्ठलें
मन ठेउनि[62] राहि[63] निर्धारिं

(SSG 296)

I fall at the feet of one
who travels to see the Lord.

Vitthal is my home,
that's where I go
in my sensibility.

My Father, the Lord of the great goddess,
my mind is made up; my mind is completely
made up.

(SSG 296)

बावनाचे संगती द्रुम भावें रातलें
सेखीं आपुलिया मुकलें जातीकुळा

लोहाचे सायास परिसेंसी फिटलें
तैसें मज केलें गोवळयाने

मेघजळ वोळे मिळें सिन्धुचिया जळा
तैसा नव्हे तो वेगळा एक होऊनि ठेला

बापरखुमादेविवरविठ्ठल नुरोचि कांहीं
उत्तम मध्यम ठाई व्यापुनि असे

(SSG 298)

Like the sandalwood tree
making trees nearby dance with fragrance,
I have lost my me-ness, my caste, my creed.

Like base metal dreaming of the philosopher's stone,
He touched me and changed me into gold.[64]

Like rain falling from dark clouds[65]
merging with the ocean's waters
losing its separate, its alone,
into the One.

High or low
He pervades all,
leaving nothing,
my Father, Lord of the great goddess.

(SSG 298)

जे ब्रह्मीं पाहतां मन न सिरे कोठें
ऐसियाचे पेठें मज उभें केलें

नावाडा श्रीरंगु जाहाला हाळुवारु
तेणें पावविला पारु ब्रह्मविद्येचा

श्रीगुरुविण सर्व शून्य हेंचि मी जाणें
तेथिचिये खुणे निवृत्तिराजु

बापरखुमादेविवरी विठ्ठलीं अनुसंधान
रात्रिदिन लीन ब्रह्मस्थिति

(SSG 299)

That Brahman,
seeing whom the mind quits bumping into things,
on that plate
He has me
standing.

Gentle is this ferryman Shreeranga,[66]
taking me across waters so rough,
reaching me to the yonder shore[67]
smoothly, lovingly.

This much I know;
it's all just for naught without the Guru.
Nivritti the King, carries the signs.

Join your mind to Vitthal,
    Lord of the great goddess;[68]
Be absorbed in Brahman
night and day.

(SSG 299)

ब्रह्माची पुतळी मीचि पैं जालों
ब्रह्मचि लेइलो अंजनगे माय

ब्रह्मचि सुख ब्रह्मपदीं पावलों
ब्रह्मसुखी निवालों निजींनिज देखा

बापरखुमादेविवरु ब्रह्मपदीं सामावला
मजसहित घेउनि गेला निजपुटीं

(SSG 301)

I have become the very image of Brahman;
I have applied the lotion of Brahman
to my eyes.

I have attained the joy that is Brahman,
attained His station.
I have attained to supreme rest
seeing myself in me.

Lord of the great goddess
has dissolved into Brahman
and taken me along
with Him.

(SSG 301)

सिद्ध सांडूनि निजबोधा गेलें
निजबोधु भुललें ब्रह्मभुली

आठवेना माझें पूर्वजन्मग्राम
अवघाचि श्रम माझा हिरोनि नेला

बापरखुमादेविवरविट्ठलें वेडावलें
आपणासहित मज ब्रह्मीं बुडविलें

(SSG 302)

From attainment [69]
into awareness of the Self;
from awareness of the Self
into the Absolute.[70]

Lost all trace
of doings, past dwellings,[71]
He stole away my entire burden.

He has driven me mad,
Lord of the great goddess,
He has drowned me in Brahman,
along with Himself.

(SSG 302)

देखावया लागी जव अनौतें पाहिलें
तव तनु मनु त्रिभुवनीं व्यापिलेंगे माये

नवलावो जालें जग हरिच होऊनि ठेलें
आठऊं विसरलें काय करूं

बापरखुमादेविवरविठ्ठलें साच केलें
लोह परिसेंसि झगटलें तैसें जालेंगे माये

(SSG 304)

I went looking for you
as one separate and different
and found you pervading everything,[72]
body and mind.

What a wondrous sight,
the world itself has become Hari.[73]
I have forgotten to remember.[74]
Now what am I to do?

Lord of the great goddess, Vitthal
has made me true.[75]
Happens when iron tangles
with philosopher's stone.

(SSG 304)

नेणते ठायीं मन पाहों गेलें
तंव मरणचि पावले जागृतीगे माये

जागृती अंतीं स्वप्न देखिलें
जागृतीं स्वप्न दोन्ही हारपले

रखुमादेविवरु मरणधरणा भ्याला
तेणें मज दाविला तेजोमय

(SSG 305)

Went looking for my mind
in the place of unknowing;
found death itself
while wide awake.

At the end of waking
I saw dreaming
and then proceeded to
lose them both.[76]

Lord of the great goddess,
Death's keeper[77]
got scared
and showed me the luminous.

(SSG 305)

मन मारुनियां मुक्त पैं केले
मीपण माझें नेलें हिरोनियां

मज लाविले चाळा लाविले चाळा
विठ्ठलुचि डोळा बैसलासे

बापरखुमादेविवरु विठ्ठलु लाघवी भला
आपरूपीं मज केला सौरसु

(SSG 306)

Killed my mind,
made me free,
stole my me-ness,
hauled it away.

He's got me hooked, all hooked,
has seated Himself in my eyes.

Trickster he, that Vitthal,
Lord of the great goddess;
sweet-talking,
made me as Himself.[78]

(SSG 306)

अगाधपण माझें अंगीं बाणलें
वरपडें देखिलें मृत्तिका लिंग

त्यासि चैतन्य नाहीं गुण नाहीं
चळण नाहीं गुण रूप नाहीं

माझ्या शरीरीं ज्योतिर्लिंग[79] उगवलें
अगाध कळविलें हस्तेंविण

बापरखुमादेविवरु ज्योतिर्लिंग विश्वनाथ
तेणें माझा मनोरथ पुरविलागे माये

(SSG 307)

My body has become saturated with the infinite.
I have seen Him in this pot of clay.[80]

Without form, consciousness, qualities, or
movement,
that flame of light is born in me.
It has made me know
that which is beyond knowing.

Lord of the great goddess,
Unborn flame, master of the universe,
has satisfied my longing.[81]

(SSG 307)

चैतन्य चोरूनि नेलें चित्त माझें सवें गेलें
पाहे तंव तन्मय जालें गे माये

देवें नवल केलें मन माझें मोहिलें
विसरु तो आठऊ जालागे माये

यासी जाणावयालागी अनुउते पाहे
तंव त्रिभुवन तन्मय जालेंगे माये

बापरखुमादेविवरें विठ्ठलरायें
माझें सबाह्याभ्यंतर व्यापिलेंगे माये

(SSG 310)

Stole my consciousness,
my mind, and me with it.
Seeing Him, I became one
with Him.

It's a miracle, what He's done,
capturing my mind.
I had forgotten;
Now I remember Him.

I went looking for Him
through the unstruck sound
and everything became
filled with Him.

Lord of the great goddess,
Vitthal the King
has filled everything—
my inside and out.

(SSG 310)

निरालंब स्तंब घातला निजयोगु
साहि वेगळेसि वो माय

आणिकां न कळे तें त्रिगुणां वेगळें
तें मज गोवळें दावियलें वो माय

दुर्घट घडतां न वर्णवे ग़ोग्यता
मज पुढारी वो माय

खुणा जरी बोलों तरी मौन्य पडलें
ते परब्रह्मीं उघडलें दिव्यचक्षु वो माय

तो चिदानंद पुतळा रखुमाई जवळा
सोइरा सकळांसहित वो माय

(SSG 319)

Pillar of life,
support of all,
Himself standing on nothing.[82]

Creating Himself in Himself,[83]
can't know Him as the other,
this one beyond knowing,
this one beyond becoming.[84]
That one[85] He showed me.

Try as you will
you can't rope Him in words,
standing as He does
right in front.

So how about some other way
like signs, allusions?

Silence!

My sight's opened
to the Absolute,
to the very core
of conscious bliss.

I have seen Him,
His enchanting form
standing by the great goddess,
beloved of all.

(SSG 319)

जन्माचें व्याज आपणचि गिळिलें
मुदलाचा ठावो नाहीं ऐसे केलें

रिणाइत नव्हे हा निर्गुणासि समंधु
येणे परमबोधु बोधविला

ऐसी आपुली साक्षी कवणें पै द्यावी
निवृत्ति म्हणे कांहीं ठायीं न ठेवीची

बापरखुमादेविवरें केला घातासु घातु
आपुला लक्षाचा लाभु वरी दिधला

(SSG 323)

I have swallowed the debt of my birth,
paid off the whole note with interest.

The unborn makes no mortgage,
it is settled with knowledge of the Self.

So how do you give witness to the Self?
Nivritti says, let go whatever could be kept.

Lord of the great goddess has joined gold to gold,
has given me the goal—
Himself.

(SSG 323)

दुरुनि येक ऋण मागावया आलें
माझें मीं पाहिलें तंव काहीं नाहीं

भीतरील माझीं पंचरत्नें नेलीं
स्वस्वरूप वाहवलीं मध्य गिळियेलें

निवृत्ति बोधें मी बोधलें
सांगतें वाहवले सर्वस्वेंसी

ऐसा रखुमादेविवरुविठ्ठलु आपण पुढारला
माझा निर्वाळा केला संसारींचा

(SSG 324)

An old debt came knocking
at the door.
I went looking for something with which to pay
but found nothing that was mine.

The five jewels are gone,
my Self is swallowed[86]
along with the center.

By Nivritti's knowledge
I too have come to know;
now everything
has been offered up.

Vitthal, Lord of the great goddess,
has moved in
resolving everything,
my whole web of fancy.[87]

(SSG 324)

तुझिया गुणासाठीं लागलों भजनापाठीं
तुझी सगुणगोठी हृदयीं वसे

मी म्हणे तें जीवन कीं निर्गुण चैतन्यघन
व्याप्य व्यापक स्थान दुजें नाहीं

विश्वाकारें जगडंबरला जो श्रुति नेति नेति म्हणोनि ठेला
हेंचि भावें विचारी भलें

परि दृष्टी सगुण हृदयींचि हेचि खुण
परि न विसंबे तुझीया पाया रया

तूं एकुची एकला बाहिजु भीतरी
कोणा द्वैतपरी सांगों बापा

म्हणोनि परापर स्थूळसूक्ष्मादि विचार
तो तुझा सगुणचि आधार मज वाटे

म्हणोनी ते तुझी बुंथी हेचि उरो आम्हां स्थिती
कीं द्वैताद्वैत भ्रांती न लगे मना

ते तुझेनि सुखें पडिपाडे आणि हें मनचि स्वयें उजाळें
तेथें थोडें बहू न निवडे ऐसें जालें

तेथें आपुलेंचि अंग विसर पडो ठेलें
शेखी सोंगची दुणावलें रया

या मनाची भ्रांती फेडावया तो तुझा सगुणभाव मज गोड
  लागे
पाहाते पाहाणियामाजि स्वयेंची विस्तारलासी कीं
  देखणेंचि होऊनी अंगें

त्रिपुटीसहित शून्याशून्य निमाले
ओंकार मार्गही न चले

रखुमादेविवरु विठ्ठले उदारे
सुख भोगिजे येणें अंगें रया

(SSG 351)

I have taken to singing your praises
because I am after your value;
your enchanting form has moved into my heart.

Is it Life that says "I"
or is it the formless dense mass of consciousness
that says so?

The dwelling and the indweller aren't two.
The one they describe as "not-this, not-this"
is the one that has become the world.
I hold this understanding
yet I can't forget your lovely form;
my heart carries one mark—your form.

You alone are, inside and out,
how can one speak of two?
Therefore, all this talk of here and yonder,
the subtle understandings of levels of being,
to me, it all rests in your form alone.

May all that is left of me be your enchanting form,
that my mind be far from the bewildering madness
 of "He is One, He is Two."

Soaked in your bliss,
bathing the mind in your brilliance,
not concerned about more or less,
one forgets one's very body.

There is no better medicine for my delusion than
your sweet form,
seeing yourself in the seen, nothing but your own
expansion, your own body.
The very triad, the void and the no-void, even the
sacred syllable Om,
all disappear here.

By the generosity of Vitthal,
the Lord of the great goddess,
feast on bliss
in your own body.

(SSG 351)

सर्व जीव तूं जालासी आपण
तरी निरय आपदा भोगिताहे कवण
परमात्मया तुमचें अविनाश स्वरूप
तरी येवढें कां कष्ट साधन
तूं अंतरीं परब्रह्म सांवळें म्हणोनि
जगत्रय व्यापिलें या ध्यानें
म्हणोनि तुमचा पुत्र जालों स्वामिया
जगाअधीन कां केलें माझें जिणें रया

तूं बाप म्हणता मी लाजिलों
लाजोनी माघारा ठेलों
एकीकडे काळ एकीकडे संसार
मध्येंचि वाटे ठेलों
ऐसिया सन्निधी तुज जवळा येवों
पाहें तंव तुझीया देवपणा भ्यालों
नादबिंदापासाव शरीर जन्मलें
असाध्य करूनी वरी साक्ष देऊनी मदामांसामाजी
वाढविलें
कर्मदेह वेचुनी सत्य सुकृतालागी उपजविलें
तरी हें दैन्य दारिद्र्य कां भोगविलें
तुझीया बापपणा बोलु लागला तरी
मज पुत्रसें वायां म्हणितलें रया

आयुष्याची गणना करूनिया प्रमाण
वरी मनुष्य देह ऐसें नाम ठेविलें
तें आयुष्य कां स्वामी तुम्ही दोंठायीं वाटिलें
अर्ध रात्रीचे अर्ध दिवसाचे निरय सत्व वेचिलें

पैल समर्थाचे बाळक रंकें गांजिलें
त्याचें थोरपण तें काय जालें रया

बांधोनी जन्म आम्हांकडे भोगविसी
आपणया मायबापा म्हणविसी
विश्व प्रसवला या जगासी
तरी आधारु आहे ऐसे अनुवादसी
जत्र जीव तत्र शिव
हे तो नये माझिया मनासी
पैल कीटकिये भृंगिये जैसी जाले
तैसें कां न करिसी आम्हासीरे

अल्प दोषासाठीं आम्हांतें दंडिसी
येवढें कैचे मंत्रसाधन जे भक्ति करूनि निरसूं तयासी
तुज देखतां काळ शरीर फाडफाडुं भक्षिताहे
कवण कां सांडिली ऐसी
जठर सीणसीण फुटतील देवा
वायां कष्टविसिल आम्हांसिरे

दर्पणीं पाहातां येकचि दिसे
तेथें अनुसारिखें कांहीं न दिसे
रविबिंब उगवलिया किरणीं प्रकाश
आस्तु जालियावरी कांहीं न दिसे
तैसे गुरुशिष्य संवादु सोहं बोध
ऐक्य जालें अभ्यासें
याहूनि जाणसी तें करि
वेळोवेळां आतां सांगों मी तें कैसें रया

यमें जाचितां कांहीं नुरे
यालागीं मुनि सेविती वनवास
खवणीक फणीक लुंचनीक वसैत
भटभराडे धाकें करिती आरामसंन्यास
योग साधावया वनवास
सेविती करिती पवनअभ्यास
इंद्रियें दंडून परतोनि गृहस्थान
न पवतीच खडु पान रसु रया

जळींचा तरंगु जळीं निमाला
तो अनुठाया वेगळा नाहीं गेला
तैसा तुजमाजी दातारा
मध्ये कां हा प्रपंच वाढविला
तूं देव आम्ही प्राकृत मनुष्यें
हा आगमु कां गमला
मज पाहतां हें अवघेंचि लटिकें
जैसें असेल तैसें सांग पां उगला

लवण पाणियांसी कीं पाणी लवणांसीं
ऐक्य जालियाविण निवडेना गुणास
लोहो लागलें परिसीं तें उठिलें कनकेंसी
बापरखुमादेविवरा विठ्ठला परियेसी
आजिपासून ये तरी तुझीच आण
पुढती न घाली न निघे गर्भवासीं रया

(SSG366)

You yourself have become us all;
why then put us through such suffering?
Nothing can touch you, no sorrow, no pain,
why then is our path of sorrow and pain?
You pervade the universe in your dark form as
    Brahman;
why then pawn me to the world, your own son?

I balked on the path and turned around ashamed, for
    I am your son.
So this is what I get? Stuck between death and this
    world of change?
I yearn to be near you but God, how your God-ness
    scares me.

You build our body from light and sound,[88]
convert it into flesh and bones,
make its origins unattainable,
and then give us a mind to see this farce.
I mortgaged my body to farm goodness and truth,
so you send me poverty in body and soul;
and if I give lip to your fatherhood
that only shows me up as son of bad blood.

You mete this life out like a miser and call it human
and then divide it into twos, days of light,
    nights of dark.
Is this a show of your power,
that the child of the king wanders the streets like a
    beggar?

You call yourself our mother and our father
and then stick us with this life of suffering;
you give birth to this world and say you are its
    support
but I see no sign of awareness that I am you.
Is it really so hard to turn us into a butterfly from
    eggs?

For paltry infractions you send us huge judgments,
so big we have to work them off with mantras and
    offerings.
Seeing you, time tears us to pieces.
Why set us such a trap?
You have us wander
from womb to womb
putting us through
pointless misery.

When you see your face in the mirror, really there is
    only one, there is no other.
When the sun rises, there is light; when it sets, there
    is nothing to see.
In the same way, from a conversation with the Guru,
one learns the secret of identity.
Well, if you know another way, why not tell?

Nothing escapes the jaws of death,
so the ascetics go into the forest,
inflict *pranayam* and yoga and god knows what,
punish their senses no end,
yet receive nothing.

The wave that rises from water disappears
into water;
it was never separate, was it?
Why then do you, our benefactor, set us up to this
market place?
You are the Lord, and we mere mortals;
why this endless game?
Look at me, tell me like it is, show me the farce of
this enterprise.

Whether salt to water or water to salt,
once they meet they are not two.
When iron touches the philosopher's stone
it wakes up to its goldness.
O bring me to Vitthal in the same way.
I put an oath unto you,
don't put me to this grindstone again.

(SSG 366)

मी माझें करूनि देह चालविसी वाया
आता जेथींचा तेथें निमोनि जाय ऐसें कीजे देवराया

जंव जंव गोड तंव तंव जाड
जाड गोड दोन्ही नको रया

त्रिगुणवोझें जडपण रचूनि लोटुनि देसी महापुरीं
आवर्त वळसा पडिलिया मग तेथें कैची असे उरी रया

ऐसें लटिकेंचि गाह्राण देवों मी किती
तुज नये काकुलती
बापरखुमादेविवरा विठ्ठला म्या तुजमाजी घेतली सुती रया

(SSG 450)

With the tools of me and mine
you run this body hapless;
I wish you'd make it
so it merges back to where it belongs.

Where there is sweet,
there is the bitter;
I want no commerce with sweet or the bitter.

You tie us hard
to becomings,[89]
drowning us
into the flood.[90]
Is there anything that escapes
the vortex of this deluge?

I keep complaining lamely, endlessly
but you, do you give a damn?
I won't quit, I hang on
to you, Vitthal, father, Lord.[91]

(SSG 450)

पैलमेरुच्या शिखरीं
एक योगि निराकारी
मुद्रा लावुनि खेंचरी
तो ब्रह्मपदीं बैसला

तेणें सांडियेली माया
त्यजयेली कंथा काया
मन गेलें विलया
ब्रह्मानंदा माझारी

अनुहत ध्वनि नाद
तो पावला परमपद
उन्मनी तुर्यांविनोदें
छंदे छंदे डोलतुसे

ज्ञानगोदावरीच्या तीरीं
स्नान केलें पाचाळेश्वरीं
ज्ञानदेवाच्या अंतरीं
दत्तात्रेय योगिया

(SSG 714)

At the vertex of yonder mountain,
stripped of form,
turned around, inward,[92]
standing in Brahman,
he moves
in the pure space of consciousness.

He has given up illusion,
given up the story of the body,
mind dissolved,
he returns to the bliss of the Absolute.

Attaining to the supreme state,
listening to the hidden waterfall [93]
having uprooted the mind in sport [94]
in the fourth,[95]
he sways in ecstasy.[96]

(SSG 714)

चहूं शून्याआरुतें महाशून्यापरुतें
सर्वांसी पहातें तेंची तें गा

दिसे तेंही शून्य पहा तेहीं शून्य
देहामाजी निरंतर भिन्न रूप

शून्य निरशून्य दोन्ही हारपलीं
तेथूनि पाहिली निजवस्तू

ध्येय ध्यान ध्याता निरसुनी तिन्ही
झालों निरंजनीं अति लीन

ज्ञानदेव म्हणे अनुभवी तो जाणें
गुरुमुखें खुण सांगितली

(SSG 801)

On this side of the four voids[97]
beyond the great void[98]
lies the One that sees all.
He is the one.[99]

Whatever is seen is only the void;
the seeing itself is the void;
taking in the body, different forms
ceaselessly.

Void, no-void both disappeared.
From there I saw the Real.[100]

Dissolved the three—seer, seen, and seeing
dissolved tracelessly into the spotless one.[101]

Jnandev says, the one who knows,[102] knows.
The Guru's word provides the clue.

(SSG 801)

अव्यक्त मसुराकार पूर्वार्ध संचलें
लक्षा सरिसें झालें लक्षासी पैं

अव्यक्त देखणें देखण्या आलें व्यक्त
पहातां व्यक्त अव्यक्त दोनी नाहीं

जागृतीच्या ठायीं निजतो सहस्रदळीं
बिंदुच्या समेळीं उच्चार होतो

ज्ञानदेव शरण निवृत्तीच्या चरणा
समजुनी खुणा तटस्थ झालों

(SSG 803)

The unmanifest packed into a mustard seed,[103]
the ultimate becomes everything seen.[104]

The manifest goes looking for the formless.
Seeing, both disappear.
Nothing left.
Neither form nor the formless.

In the place of waking he rests,[105]
sleeping in the thousand-petaled lotus,
from the bindu comes expression, sound.[106]

Jnandev takes refuge at Nivritti's feet.
Seeing the signs,
becomes still.[107]

(SSG 803)[108]

आकाशासी गुंफा अंत नाहीं जिचा
शोध करा तिचा सर्वभावें

अनंत ब्रह्मांडाचा खेळ जिच्या योगें चाले
चांग्यासी मिनलें तयां ठायीं

गुंफेच्या आधारें चंद्र सूर्य चालती
विश्रांतिसी येती तये जवळी

ज्ञानदेव नयन धरितां समभावें
सोहं स्वरूप भावें लाधलेंसें

(SSG 805)

Cave without end, like unto the sky,
seek it through every *bhava*.[109]

One that runs the play of the universe,
that's where Changya found it.[110]

The sun and the moon
move under her power;
it is here they come
to pause and rest.

Jnandev says, holding equal vision,
find your nature, *So'ham*, "That I am."

(SSG 805)

षट्चक्रें बंद निघूनियां गेलीं
पाहों जो लागलीं तयां गांवा

निरंजन सभराभरीत वस्तू कोंदली
साक्षत्वासी आली आत्मदशा

वृत्ति झेंपावली आनंद झाला सैरा
सत्रावी येरझारा करी जेथें

ज्ञानदेव म्हणे लक्ष लावीं आकाशीं
ब्रह्म पावसि लौकरी तूं

(SSG 806)

The six wheels packed up and left [111]
as I gazed at that city.

The immaculate substance fills everything
to the brim.
The state of the Self stands right in front.

The tendencies of the mind have packed up and left;
bliss rains and rains;
that One, the seventeenth, visits and plays here.[112]

Jnandev says, gaze upon the sky,[113]
and find the Real, just like that.[114]

(SSG 806)

नयनाचे शेजारीं दशवें द्वार बापा
एक मार्ग सोपा बोलतसें

आधारीं पवन अपान विराजे
आंगुळें चार साजे तयां ठायीं

मणिपुर चक्र नाभिस्थान कमळ
सहा अंगुळांचा खेळ असे तेथे

वायुचक्र अनुहात हृदय असे एक
प्राणासी निःशंक जेथे नेई

अग्नीचक्र भ्रुवांग शोभतें प्रकाशत्व
प्राणासी उलथावे तयावरी

सहस्रदळीं ब्रह्मरंध्र शोभतसे निळें
प्रकाशाचे उमाळे जेथे असती

ज्ञानदेव म्हणे ऐका प्राणायाम
या अभंगी निःसीम अर्थ झाला

(SSG 807)

Door near the eyes,
the tenth door,[115]
let me tell you of the path to it,
the easy path.[116]

In the *aadhaara,* the root,
lies the living air, the inhalation.
Above it, at four fingers,
the *manipura* complex at the belly button.[117]

Room to play
for six more fingers
to the wind complex at the heart,
anahat, the unstruck.
Take your life force there; [118]
do not hesitate.

The vortex of fire at the brows[119]
wears a glorious light.
Pull your breath there, inverted.

In the thousand petals[120]
is the gorgeous blue;
fountain of illumination
the opening to Brahman.[121]

Hear ye all, says Jnandev:
in this *abhanga*
is a clear explanation of *pranayama,*
    the control of breath.

(SSG 807)

सोहंकारी माया लक्षा आणीं देहीं
निरंजनीं पाहीं मायाकार

निर्गुण सगुण माया तेची खरी
प्रसऊनी निर्धारी वांझ असे

ज्ञानदेव म्हणे मज माया कृपाळु झाली
तिणें उजळली माझी काया

(SSG 809)

Go see within your body,
Soham, That I am,
and within it, the force of Maya.
See the form of Maya
in the formless.

She is the real one
formless, with form
forever birthing,
forever barren.

Jnandev says,
Maya has taken mercy on me;
filled my body
with light.

(SSG 809) [122]

आकाशीं मळा लाविला वा एक
वांझेचें बाळक शिंपीतसे

अग्नीकुंड मनें बाळकें निर्मिलें
प्रत्ययासी देखिलें मीया लागीं

ज्ञानदेव म्हणे उफराटें पहातां
सर्व सौख्यदाता निवृत्ति एक

(SSG 810)

Son of a barren woman[123]
watering a garden in the sky.

The boy forges a fire-pit
with his mind
and goes on gazing
with his eyes.

Jnandev says,
when you turn around and look backwards,
you see the giver of all that is worthwhile,
that one Nivritti.

(SSG 810)

पहा त्रिभुवनीं न दिसे बाइये
नयनांजनीं पाहें आत्मरूप

मन बुद्धि चित्त अंत:करण जाण
या वेगळें निर्वाण ब्रह्म तेंचि

ज्ञानदेवा ब्रह्म लाधलें अवचटें
उन्मनीचा घांट चढतांची

(SSG 811)

Look as you might
wherever,[124]
you can't see Him,
anywhere.
See Him as your own Self,
filling your eyes with subtle vision.

Here you have the mind
and its many forms,[125]
and then there is Brahman, the Absolute, the free.[126]

Jnandev climbed the mountain of no-mind [127]
and found Him unexpectedly, [128]
just like that.

(SSG 811)

आत्मज्ञान जया न देखा निजदृष्टी
तया नरा गोष्टी करूं नये

तुर्यारूपें जाण प्रभा हे निःसिम
तया परत राम असे बापा

ज्ञानदेवा गुज दाविलें गुरूनें
मनें अनन्ये कल्पीतांची

(SSG 812)

Don't prate, don't tell stories
if you haven't seen the Self with your own eyes.[129]

There is this light,
clear, without limit,
dwelling in the form of the fourth,[130]
and beyond it the Lord, Rama.

The Guru revealed to me the secret
as soon as I went to him with a one-pointed mind.

(SSG 812)

आत्मा एक बाई स्थिरचरव्यापक
सृष्टी तैसी देख एकलीच

पंचमहाभूतें व्यापूनी निराळा
सौंदर्य पुतळा काळाबाई

ज्ञानदेव ध्यान धरिलें पुढती
त्रैलोक्याची वस्ती असे जेथें

(SSG 813)

That one Self pervades
all things moving and unmoving.
See all of creation as such.

This dark one,
gorgeous mass of beauty,
fills all yet stands apart, [131]
aloof, beyond, separate.

Jnandev holds Him in front in awareness,
this one in whom all is.[132]

(SSG 813)

अकारी अर्धमात्रा कवण रीति दिसे
उकारीही घुसे[133] कवणे परी

मकारी संयुक्त झाली कैशापरी
अर्धमात्रेवरी अर्धमात्रा

अर्धमात्रेचा अर्थ अवचटची दिसे
गुरुगम्य सोय जाणती पैं

ज्ञानदेवें अर्थ शोधुनी घेतला
महाशून्यीं संचला निवृत्तिराज

(SSG 814)

How does one see
the half utterance,[134]
the one that holds
everything?[135]

The meaning comes unexpectedly
when you find the way
the Guru knows.

Jnandev did his research
and found the meaning.
King Nivritti fills the great void.

(SSG 814)

शून्य हे चार महाशून्य दिसतसें
निजरंग वसे सर्व त्यांत

ऐसा रंग जया लाधतांचि पाहे
मनाची ही सोइ हारपली

ज्ञानदेवाचा बोल बोलण्याचें रूप
निवृत्तिस्वरूप सर्वत्र हें

(SSG 815)

Here are the four voids
and the great void beyond.[136]
The color of the Self
drenches them all.

A color when you touch,
the mind loses its
bearings.

Jnandev's words
embody the form;
the form that everywhere
is Nivritti.

(SSG 815)

शून्याचें जे बीज योगीयांचें गुज
स्वानंदाचें निज ब्रह्म रया

त्रिगुण त्रिविध तो सच्चिदानंद
शब्दाचा अनुवाद नसे जेथें

ज्ञानदेव म्हणे सद्‌गुरु जाणती
इतरांची वृत्ति चालेचीना

(SSG 816)

The source of the void[137]
is the yogi's secret,
the essence of one's bliss, the Brahman.

That one, sat-chit-ananda[138]
where words fall silent,
takes on the three-fold form.[139]

Jnandev says, the Guru knows
that which is simply
incomprehensible
otherwise.[140]

(SSG 816)

गगनमंडळीं नारी सुकुमार दिसे
तिन्ही लोक वसे तिचे उदरीं

परादी वाचा तन्मय ते झाली
साक्षीत्वासी आली ब्रह्मरंध्री

ज्ञानदेव म्हणे नयनांतील ज्योती
पाहातां वृत्ति हरे विषयांची

(SSG 821)

Enchanting maiden in the space of the sky,[141]
all three worlds dwell in her womb;
at one with words, said and unsaid [142]
she comes as the witness,
    at the door of Brahman.[143]

Jnandev says, the tendency to wander
is lost when you see the light in the eyes.

(SSG 821)

सकार हकारीं नाडी दिसती कैशा
उलटल्या दशदिशा अमुपचि

सूक्ष्म मूळ सर्व बीजाचा उद्‌भव
हाची अनुभव देहामध्यें

समान जैसा अर्क स्थिरचर एकला
आत्मा हा संचला तैशा परि

ज्ञानदेव म्हणे याहुनी आणिक
बोलाचे कवतुक जेथ नाही

(SSG 827)

See the subtle channels
in the sounds of *sa* and *ha*; [144]
see the ten directions turned inside out, [145]
unlimited, unfathomable.

See in your own body [146]
the subtle origin of all,
the creation of all seeds.

The equal, the even, the one essence,
the Self pervades all;
all that moves and doesn't.[147]

Says Jnandev,
this is the limit of speech.
It goes no farther.

(SSG 827)

काळा पुरुष तो हा गगनात जो नांदे
अनुभवाच्या भेदें भेदला जो

भेदून अभेद अभेदूनि भेद
सच्चिदानंद जेथ नाहीं

ज्ञानदेव म्हणे तेथें अक्षय राहिला
आत्मा म्यां पाहिला या दृष्टिसी

(SSG 829)

That dark one who revels in the sky,[148]
discern Him with the power of experience.

Discern Him, know no-difference,
otherwise there is only the other, only the lack
of the Real.[149]

After all is said and done, only the imperishable
remains.
Jnandev sees Him with his own eyes.

(SSG 829)

विश्व ब्रह्म भासे ऐक्य येतां देहीं
अनुहातीं पाहीं अपार नाद

देखिला परी संयोगें व्यापला
विश्व तरीच झाला बाइयानो

पिंड ब्रह्मांडाचा विस्तार विस्तारला
माझा मीच झाला कोणपरी

ज्ञानदेव म्हणे ह्या अर्थाची सोय
धरी माझी माय मुक्ताबाई

(SSG 830)

Once the body touches oneness,
the whole world appears as Brahman,
an infinite expanse of the unstruck sound
in the heart.[150]

You see Him,
and in that union, He expands into the universe.

All is me, all is mine.
Jnandev says, Muktabai holds this
in the palm of her hand.[151]

(SSG 830)

गुजगुजीत रूप सावळे सगुण
अनुभवितां मन वेडें होय

भ्रमर गुंफा ब्रह्मरंध्र तें सुरेख
पहाता कौतुक त्रैलोकीं

आनंद स्वरूप प्रसिद्ध देखिलें
निजरूप संचलें सर्वां ठायीं

ज्ञानदेव म्हणे या सुखाची गोडी
अनुभवाची आवडी सेवीं रया

(SSG 831)

The poor mind goes mad
when it experiences that dark enchanting form.
There is no other sight so lovely.

At that secret entrance, at that opening into
Brahman,[152]
I have seen something; I have seen that famous form
of love,[153]
I have seen the essence of the Self pervading all.[154]

Jnandev says, this is the experience;
this is the sweet joy I savor.

(SSG 831)

सहस्र दळ बिंदु त्यांत तेज दिसे
तें हो काय ऐसें सांगा मज

जेथ नाम रूप वर्ण नाहीं बारे
तें हें रूप बारे चैतन्य बा

ज्ञानदेव म्हणे अनुभवाची खूण
जाणे तो सुजाण अनुभविया

(SSG 832)

Point of light blazing inside a thousand-petals,
what light is this, pray tell?

No name, no form, no color here, friend.
This is the conscious[155] one, the free.

Jnandev says, only that fortunate one
    who has experienced
understands.[156]

(SSG 832)

कोणाचें हें रूप देह हा कोणाचा
आत्माराम साचा सर्व जाणे

मी तूं हा विचार विवेकें शोधावा
गोविंद हा घ्यावा याच देहीं

ध्येय ध्याता ध्यान त्रिपुटीं वेगळां
सहस्रदळीं उगवला सूर्य जैसा

ज्ञानदेव म्हणे नयनांतील रूप
या नांव चित्पद तुम्ही जाणा

(SSG 833)

This form and this body,
who do they belong to?
The Self knows all.

With great care, ponder and examine the thought:
    I and thou;[157]
find Him within your own body.

Beyond the threesome of the seer, seen, and seeing,
He rises from the thousand petals
like the rising sun.

Says Jnandev, see that beauteous form in the eyes?
Know that one to be the conscious.[158]

(SSG 833)

डोळियांत डोळा काळियांत काळा
देखण्या निराळा निळारूप

ब्रह्म तत्व जाणें ज्योतिरूपें सगळा
ज्योतीही वेगळा ज्योती वसे

ज्ञानदेव म्हणे देवा ऐसी ज्योती
अर्धमात्रा उत्पत्ति सर्वांजीवां

(SSG 834)

Eye of the eye, dark of the dark,
that blue one is something to see.

Know Brahman as everything, through the flame,[159]
different from the flame, dwelling in the flame.

Jnandev says, O Lord, such is its glory[160]
all beings arise from its mere flicker.[161]

(SSG 834)

सद्गुरु निवृत्ति दिसतो घनदाट
सुषुप्तीचा घांट वेधतांची

आत्मामाया शिवशक्तीचे हें रूप
दिसतें चिद्रूप अविनाश

ज्ञानदेव चढे ऐसी वाट देख
आकाशीं असे मुख तिचें कैसें

(SSG 835)

Cross the walls of slumber[162]
and see that Nivritti fills everything to the brim.

This play of the Self, of the Lord and His power,[163]
appears as the eternal, the undying, the conscious.[164]

Jnandev says, go and see
its face in the sky of consciousness.[165]

(SSG 835)

जडांतील शुद्धांश कौतुकें रिघाला
निवृत्तीनें दाविला कृपा करूनि

अनुहात भेद दाविला कृपेनें
सर्व हें चैतन्य गमलें तेव्हां

ज्ञानदेव नमनीं निवृत्तीचे पदीं
आनंद ब्रह्मपदीं एक झाला

(SSG 842)

Nivritti took mercy on me,
showed me the pure portion of inert things,
as if in play.

He favored me with the secret of the unstruck sound.
He showed me that all was marvelously conscious.

Jnandev merely bowed at Nivritti's feet
and became one with Brahman, the abode of bliss.

(SSG 842)

प्रणवासी रूप नाहीं काहीं छाया
दशवे द्वारीं मूळमाया असे कीं रे

सहस्रदळीं वृत्ति लावितां निःशंक
मनासी भवासी ऐक्यता तेथें

ज्ञानदेव म्हणे या परतें नाहीं
बोलण्याची सोयी अनुभवी जाणे

(SSG 847)

That original sound[166] without form,
without shadow,
source of the entire play[167]
is at the tenth gate.[168]

If you engage your mind at the thousand petals,
your mind will unite with the world.[169]

Jnandev says, there is nothing beyond this.
Only one who has experienced, understands.

(SSG 847)

प्रणवाचें रूप कोणें देहें देखिलें
निवृत्तिनें दाविले याच देहीं

सकार हकार तुर्या उन्मनी भेद
अभेदुनी भेद केले मज

ज्ञानदेव म्हणे प्रणवाची खोली
अक्षरींची बोली देह सार

(SSG 851)

How many get to see the truth in this body? [170]
Nivritti showed it to me.

He showed me the no-mind, the fourth state;[171]
the inhalation and exhalation of letters
he showed me. [172]

The secret of the non-dual he showed me.

Jnandev says, letters are the essence of the body;
they express the depths of *pranava*.[173]

(SSG 851)

अमृताची क्षीर ब्रह्मांडभुवनीं
पाहाती त्रिभुवनीं नवल झालें

नाद विंदा भेटी झाली कवण्या रीती
शुद्ध ब्रह्म ज्योती संचलीसे

प्रकृति पुरुष शिव शक्ति भेद
त्याचे शरीरीं द्वंद्व देह जाणा

ज्ञानदेव म्हणे पिंडीं शोध घ्यावा
ब्रह्मांडीं पाहावा ब्रह्म ठसा

(SSG 852)

All of creation
swims in the nectar of immortality;
what a wondrous sight it is.

Meeting the conscious point and the sound,[174]
filled with the pure light of Brahman.[175]

The world and its witness, the holy and its power,[176]
their two-ness is reflected in you;
they make your body.

Jnandev says, look for yourself in your own body.
The whole world bears the stamp of its maker.

(SSG 852)

आत्माराम देखे सहस्रदळावरी
उन्मनी हे पाही आरुते तेहीं

चक्षुचे अंतरीं चक्षु देखे पूर्ण
हेचि कीरे खुण तुझें ठायीं

मी ब्रह्म सोहं ज्ञानपद तें साजिरें
ते ठायीं निधारिं तुझा तूंचि

बापरखुमादेवीवरा तुझा तूं आपण
सर्व हें चैतन्य तुझे ठायीं

(SSG 865)

See the Self in the thousand petals.
Turn your mind inside out.[177]
See Him at hand.

"Inside the eye is the perfect Eye"[178]
is all the help you need.

"I am Brahman, I am the absolute,
I am the station of knowledge, That I am."
Go stalk it with resolution.
You are it, it is yours.[179]

O my dear one, Lord of the great goddess,
all that is conscious, that is free is you.[180]

(SSG 865)

औटपीठातळीं तेज गुजगुजीत
चारी देह तेथ साक्ष पाहा

अवस्था हे चारी संयोगची एक
शून्य जें निःशंक आत्मज्योती

ज्ञानदेवा बाई निवृत्ति वदविता
त्याचे चरणीं हीताहीत झालें

(SSG 866)

At the place
between the eyes [181]
lies this enchanting blaze;
watch your four bodies from there.[182]

These four states are a happen-chance;
only the light of the Self is the unconditioned,
the void.

When Nivritti spoke,
Jnandev attained everything
at his feet.

(SSG 866)

शून्याचें भुवनीं स्वरूप अविनाश
प्रणवीं पुरुष दिसतसे

निळारंग देखें सर्वांचे देखणीं
चैतन्य भुवनीं समरस

ज्ञानदेवा ध्यान सच्चिदानंदाचें
सर्व ब्रह्म साचे येणें येथें

(SSG 867)

In the palace of nothingness
lives the imperishable Self;[183]
see the primal Being inside *pranava*, Om.

All is blue, all seeing is blue,
all is steeped in the supremely conscious.

By contemplation of that *sat-chit-ananda,*
that Real, the conscious, the blissful,
bring the Absolute home.[184]

(SSG 867)

औट पिठावरी निरंतर देश
तेथ मी जगदीश असे बाई

त्रिकुटाचा फेरा टाकीला माघारा
अर्धमात्रेवरा वरी गेलों

अर्धनारी पुरुष एकरूप दीसे
तेंचि ब्रह्म ऐसें जाण बाई

ज्ञानदेवी शून्य नयनीं देखिलें
सर्वत्रीं संचलें शून्य एक

(SSG 875)

Space nestled between the eyes,[185]
its expanse knows no bounds.
I am that Lord, that's where I live.

I have passed the space of the triangle.[186]
Beyond the half-syllable have I gone.[187]

When you see that one form, half male, half female,
know it to be Brahman.

Jnandev says, I have seen the void
    with my own eyes; [188]
that void fills all.

(SSG 875)

मीच माझा डोळा मीच शून्यांत निळा
माझा मी वेगळा तयामध्यें

उफराटी दृष्टी लाविता नयनीं
ते दृष्टीची वाणी किंचित ऐका

उफराटी दृष्टि देखे उन्मनीवरी
तेव्हां निर्विकारी मीच मग

ज्ञानदेव म्हणे देहा डोळां दिठी
पाहातां सर्व सृष्टि निवृत्ती एका

(SSG 887)

I am my own eye.
I'm the blue in the void.
I am separate
from it all.

Turn your vision around,
listen a bit to what it says.

When sight turns around
and sees no-mind [189]
then it sees only
the formless I.

Jnandev says,
see the body, see the eyes,
see that all of creation is Nivritti.

(SSG 887)

निळें हें व्योम निळें हें सप्रेम
निळेपणें सम आकारलें

नीळवर्ण ब्रह्म नीळवर्ण कर्म
नीळवर्ण आश्रम गुरु देखे

निळेपणें वर्तो निळेपणें खातों
नीळपण पाहातो निळेपणें

ज्ञानदेव आला नीळवर्ण शाळा
निळेपण गोंवळा रातलीये

(SSG 30)

Blue space, blue with love,
equality made of blue.

Blue, Absolute,[190]
doing, blue;
Guru's place—well, that is blue too.

Eating blue, doing blue, seeing blue, being blue.

Jnandev has come to the school of blue.
Stuck on the color blue.[191]

(SSG 30)

कांहीं न करिजे ते तुझी सेवा
कांही नव्हेसि तें तूं देवा

नेणिजे तें तुझें रूप
जाणिजे तितुकें पाप गा देवा

स्तुति करणें ते तुझी निंदा
स्तुति जोगा नव्हेसि गोविंदा

बापरखुमादेविवरा विठ्ठला
येवढा साभिलाषु कां दाविला

(SSG 360)

Doing nothing is to serve you,
being no-thing is to be you.[192]

Not knowing is your very form,
knowing itself is the great sin.

Praising you is to insult you, O Govinda,
No catching *you* in words of praise.

Vitthal, Lord of the great goddess,
why show us all these desires?[193]

(SSG 360)

Notes

In citing works in the notes, short titles have generally been used. Works frequently cited have been identified by the following abbreviations:

DMS: Sakhare, Dada Maharaj. *Shree Jnaneshwar Maharaj Saartha Gaathaa.* Pune: 1995.

PNJ: *Saartha Sri Jnandeva Abhanga Gaathaa,* P. N. Joshi, Pune: 1969.

SSG: Joshi, Kashinath Ananta, ed. *Sakala Sant Gaathaa, Vol I.* Pune: 1975.

1. Madhav: A name of Krishna, or Vitthal. The text says "is good" or "is better."

2. This last line is Jnaneshwar's primary signature, the one he uses the most often: *Baap Rakhuma-devi-varu*: "(O) Father, husband (or Lord) of Goddess Rakhuma," or sometimes just *Rakhuma-devi-varu*. Rakhuma is Laxmi, the consort of Vitthal (or Vishnu). We generally translate this as "My Father, Lord of the great goddess," or simply, "Lord of the great goddess."

   The other signature Jnaneshwar often uses is "*Jnandev mhane,*" or "*mhane Jnandev,*" or its variations, meaning "says Jnandev." Sometimes it is simply *Jnandev* or *Jnandev* in a declension, and occasionally "Nivritti-das," servant of Nivritti.

3. Images like this show Jnaneshwar's deep connection to the tradition. See, e.g., the *Mundaka Upanishad*: "As from a blazing fire, sparks in its likeness spring forth by the thousands, so beings spring forth from the imperishable." However, he always has a fresh way of expressing what is deeply rooted in tradition.

4. We use this unusual word, "un-form," to try to reflect Jnaneshwar's use of an unusual word, *aguna,* for the formless, rather than the usual *nirguna*.

5. Nanda is the adopted father of Krishna, (and therefore ultimately, Vitthal).

   Jnaneshwar often uses the term *maaye* or *maay,* meaning "O Mother," as an affectionate way to address the unspecified listener. We couldn't find anything reasonably equivalent that would make sense in contemporary English, and have simply omitted it.

6. There is frequent reference in Jnaneshwar's poetry to Vitthal's *darkness*. This is a direct reference to his dark, black form. However, it is a veiled reference to his being pure mystery. The god-head, pure consciousness, is ever present and is always a wondrous mystery. There is nothing in Him that can be captured, whether in words or image. He is also just beyond the darkness of deep sleep, in the form of *turya*, the fourth state, or rather *turya-teeta*, beyond the fourth. But he can't be approached except *through* darkness. That darkness will lead directly to Him. To Jnaneshwar, of course, he is the Beloved.

7. DMS and PNJ have the word *vyoma*, *space* or *void*, inserted before "offering." In that case the last line would read literally, "therefore everywhere void offered." PNJ translates this as the darkness filling space. The syntax is ambiguous, and many meanings are possible. The verse could very well be *interpreted* (not translated) as: "the dark, unfathomable form fills everything. It is like the void. It fills the void. Everything we do is void and is an offering to that void."

8. *saangitalaa:* said or spoke. The couplet literally says "What to do, O mother, Krishna the dark; Nivritti spoke the question." The couplet speaks of his total immersion in Krishna's form, an immersion that came from Nivritti revealing the secret.

9. The last line literally says "bed Self bliss Krishna," which we would expand as "resting on a bed of the bliss of the Self who is Krishna."

10. *svayambhu,* "unborn," written by Jnaneshwar here as *svayambha,* is literally *self-born* or *self-manifested.*

11. The word is *chaitanya,* which means consciousness or awareness. However, in the Shaivite tradition, which Jnaneshwar is heir to, *chaitanya* is more dynamic than either consciousness or awareness. Chaitanya involves not only consciousness, but also absolute freedom, which is its nature. See, e.g., Jaidev Singh's *Siva Sutras.*

12. Original is *Jiva-shiva,* i.e., "(from) the individual self (to) the supreme Self."

13. The word is *sahaj.* This is an important word in this tradition. *Sahaj* means natural or simple. The truth is natural and simple, not complicated or twisted. Those who know the truth are also natural and simple.

14. The "devotee" is actually "Pundalik" in the text. Pundalik's devotion was responsible for bringing Vitthal to Pandharpur. Pundalik was engrossed in service to his parents. His selfless service pulled the Lord to him like a magnet, unasked, where He stands, as Vitthal, to this day. The name Pundalik is imprinted as deeply in the minds of the Marathi people as the name Vitthal itself.

15. The "inner essence of creation" is literally "Brahman, the self of the creator."

    "By all" is literally "by all gods from Brahma, the creator, on."

16. Literally, "different from the *trikuta." Trikuta* is the triangle in the *sahasrar,* the highest spiritual center.

17. His form is the devotee's Love for the supreme. So we could also say "His form is Love."

18. Vitthal stands on a brick that Pundalik offered him to stand on.

19. DMS reads आत्मा

20. Jnaneshwar uses a wonderful word *chitta-rasa*, which could be translated as the "juice of the mind." *Rasa* can mean juice, relish, inclination, sentiment, delight, essence, and many more things.

21. The original seems to say "takes support in Jnaneshwar, fully entering."

22. The text says "by stirring the twenty-one." The twenty-one clearly seems to imply the world, implying he was "sleeping, or lost, in the twenty-one and is now awake." It is not clear just what Jnaneshwar had in his mind using twenty-one. According to DMS, twenty-one refer to the number of *tattvas*, or principles; but the numbers, counting prakriti, and not counting purusha, should add up to twenty-four in the Sankhya system. The "waking up" is *nihshabdin*–either *without words*, or *into the wordless*. This is done with *fourteen*, in the text. DMS considers that to be the fourteen branches of knowledge, or *vidyas*.

23. The word Jnaneshwar uses is *sleeping*. The way he uses it is a bit more powerful than what may be conveyed by *resting*. *Resting* may still carry some individual effort whereas the intent is that Vitthal does this for him, the way a mother would do for her child. "Resting in Himself" could also be "Resting in myself."

24. The tiny spark given by the Guru spreads into the entire field, opening into the space of consciousness, decked with the flowers of sadhana, practice. The way of divine enjoyment is different from sensory enjoyment: the more you savor it, the more it increases. The mind, which may just as well run from the Lord as to Him, is given no choice: its fabric, its "knots" (*manachiye gunti*), are steeped in these flowers, and left at Vitthal's feet. Both the mind and the bounty received from the Lord are offered back to him.

25. *Govinda,* knower of the senses, and *Narayana,* lord of men, are both names of Krishna, or Vitthal. The text literally says "there is more of Him left after filling the universe."

26. Literally, lotus.

27. The text says "seventeenth," which represents the state beyond the sixteen *kalaas,* forms, of the world.

28. The text says, "the (fortune) lines of knowledge have blossomed."

29. *Jnana* - diminutive of *Jnaneshwar.*

30. *bhava.* See note 35.

31. There is a double entendre on Nivritti. The mind has been "unburdened," or "has been made into Nivritti," the Guru.

32. *Nema,* which we have translated as "unmistakable," could also be *exact* or *precise.*

    The last two lines could also be: "Nivritti bestowed upon Jnandev the supreme experience, perfect peace, and forgiveness," i.e., Jnandev now forgives all.

33. SSG has रयनि rather than गगनीं.

34. This could also be translated as "see *paraa*" or *"see with paraa."* In the latter case, it would be *"see with paraa vani,"* the subtlest form of speech.

35. *bhavana* (and *bhava*) is some sort of an amalgam of feeling, intention, contemplation, concentration, and becoming. It is active. It probably can't be translated into English.

36. The word used "manifestation" is *Vaishnavi Maya*, supreme illusory manifestation of the divine.

37. *Uparam* is to stop or end. The line could mean "by mastering the void, the no-void, and stopping," or "by mastering the void and the no-void through stopping," or "by attaining the no-void within the void, stopping."

38. *jeeva*, the individual self, usually at odds with *Shiva*, has made friends with the latter, the universal unitary Self of all. They are sitting next to each other in a feast.

39. Literally, "gave equality awareness to the entire body."

40. *sattva*, *rajas*, and *tamas* of prakriti.

41. "In the pot and the temple."

42. Literally, "Screams His name unexpectedly, behind and in front."

43. "shown my eyes."

44. The word *nivritti* literally means "the state of complete detachment." Here we see again

Jnaneshwar's use of paradoxes to jolt the mind beyond itself.

45. Jnaneshwar simply says "enjoys, giving up body consciousness." Presumably it means "he enjoys the bliss of the Self (or the bliss of everything), giving up body-consciousness."

46. Literally, "Nivritti has cooled the three fires, O mother."

47. Literally, "knowable through the Guru."

48. The line could also be interpreted as "there is no me left."

49. DMS and PNJ have *aise naahi kele*. In that case, the line would be interpreted as "this is how the King Nivritti made me into nothing," or perhaps, "… took away everything, all that was the other."

50. Namdev was a contemporary of Jnaneshwar. Originally a mad lover of the form of Vitthal and Vitthal only, another contemporary Visoba Khechar showed him that Brahman, the absolute, lives everywhere, not just in the form of Vitthal.

    The ending of this line could also be "held Him in his heart as the essence of life (*prana-linga*)."

51. There is another line here: "We'll show you the form and formless themselves."

52. Jnaneshwar uses the terms *anubhava* and *svanubhava* here. *Anubhava* is experience. *Svanubhava* is self-experience or own-experience or experience of the Self. Translated literally, the couplet would be: "Where there is no experience, that you must see; remain, you, in Self-experience, by yourself."

53. This is a reference to the *ida* and *pingala naadis* merging into the *sushumna,* the central subtle channel.

54. Literally, "such a one is a *Yogeshwar,* lord of Yogis"

55. "substance" is *vastu,* reality.

56. Hari is another name of Krishna or Vitthal.

57. Literally, "all holy places dwell in the feet of Nivritti." The holy places, *teerthas,* usually involve a river, and the second line uses that to say "taking my mind to dive in them." Hence we use "rivers" for *teertha.*

58. Or perhaps "has become one with the One."

59. Literally, "the three worlds."

60. "Lord's dwelling" is Pandharpur, the abode of Vitthal; *mahera* is mother's home, where "I will go to meet mine."

61. Literally, "I shall report my well-being in Brahman."

62. SSG repeats मन ठेउनि. This appears to be a typo, and is corrected in DMS and PNJ.

63. PNJ uses राहिलें.

64. "He" is *Govalaa,* meaning Gopal or Hari.

65. Literally, "wet rain."

66. Another name of Vitthal.

67. Literally, "yonder shore of the knowledge of Brahman."

68. "Join" is literally *anusandhaana,* which is a combination of aiming, joining, attending.

69. Text says from "giving up *siddha,* went to awareness of the Self." Siddha (usually written as *siddhi*) here means attainment. DMS and PNJ interpret it as worldly attainment. We prefer to see it simply as attainment, worldly or spiritual.

70. Original could be translated as "forgetting the awareness of the Self into the maze (or forgetfulness) of Brahman."

71. Literally, "forgot the village of past life." The poem carries a theme of forgetting.

72. Literally, "the three worlds."

73. Another name of Vitthal.

74. Because I have forgotten duality. Also, because "the light of the Self is ever new" so there is nothing to remember. See *Jnaneshwari* VI-23.

75. This could be "redeemed me."

76. See *Katha Upanishad,* 2-1-4, "at the end of waking, at the end of dreaming, that one that sees them both."

77. Jnaneshwar uses a very unusual term here, *marana-dharanaa,* holder or keeper of death.

78. "Trickster" is *laghavi,* deceitful, skillful, awesome or amazing. DMS translates this as "indulgent." In that case, it could be translated as "Vitthal, Lord of the great goddess / indulgent that he is / made me into himself / in sweet gift."

79. ज्योतिलिंग in SSG and DMS.

80. This could also be "wretched pot of clay."

81. Craving, desires.

82. *niralamba,* without support.

83. *nija-yogu,* own yoga.

84. साहि वेगळेसि means "different from the six shastras, (philosophies)." त्रिगुणा वेगळे means "separate from the three gunas." We have translated the two as "beyond knowing, beyond becoming."

85. Literally, Krishna, as Gopal, the cow herder.

86. The "five jewels" are the five senses.

"Self" is *sva-svaroopa.*

87. *samsara.*

88. *nada* and *bindu.*

89. Literally, the *gunas.*

90. The *mahapoor,* great deluge (of *samsaar,* the ocean of change).

91. There is the usual signage, "to you O Vitthal, father, Lord of the great goddess."

92. *khechari mudra.*

93. *anahata,* unstruck sound.

94. *unmani,* mind.

95. The "fourth" is the fourth state of consciousness, *turya* or *turiya,* (from *chaturtha,* "the fourth." The individual being shuttles helplessly between the three normal states: waking, dream, and deep sleep. Beyond these is the Witness, the state of *awareness,* which penetrates them all and is beyond them all. The man of knowledge knows and lives in *turya,* or actually *turya-teeta,* beyond the fourth, in the state of

pure being-consciousness, i.e., being, which is the same as consciousness.

96. We have omitted the last verse: "The supreme yogi Dattatreya (an amalgam of Brahma, Vishnu and Mahesh, the triple deities of creation, and a Lord of Yoga)/bathing on the banks of the river of knowledge/lives within Jnaneshwar."

97. According to DMS, these are the four states of consciousness, waking, dreaming, sleeping, and witnessing. Brahman, the Real, lies beyond these, as well as more at hand than these.

98. Jnaneshwar uses the term *mahashunya*.

99. Or more literally, "That is That."

100. *nija vastu,* reality.

101. *niranjan.*

102. *anubhavi,* "one who has experienced," in the sense of an enduring knowing.

103. The yogis see the supreme power as condensed into a dynamic blue mass of consciousness, size of a mustard seed, the seed of the universe.

104. This could be "attention becomes everything attended to." The word is *laksha,* which could be either the goal or attention.

105. During the waking state, one is asleep to one's true nature. See, e.g., Raman Maharshi, *Spiritual Teaching*.

106. The *bindu*, point, is the dense mass of consciousness; from it comes *ucchaar*, expression, utterance, or sound.

107. The text says "understanding the signs (*khuna*, either "pointing outs" or "signs").
"Everything becomes still." The word is *tatastha*, even, equal, perfectly still.

108. This abhanga and #807 are examples of yogic experiences and stages densely packed into a single poem.

109. *bhava* is feeling, inclination, contemplation, approach. See note 35.

110. Refers to Changdev, the yogi, who became Jnaneshwar's disciple.

111. The six *chakras* below the seventh, or highest chakra.

112. The "seventeenth one," see note 27;.
"visits and plays" could also be "comes and goes."

113 The sky of consciousness.

114. The "Real" is *Brahman*, the absolute. Having reached the final abode, Brahman, the "city," the six wheels—the lower six centers of consciousness, the centers of manifestation—have been left behind; there is nothing, no tendencies of the mind (*Vrittis*), to diminish the bliss of the state of the Self, the immaculate one, that is now seen to fill everything.

115. *brahma-randhra.* It is the tenth door, the one beyond the nine gates of the senses in the body.

116. Jnaneshwar calls this *pantha-raaj*, the king of paths, in the sixth chapter in *Jnaneshwari*, and provides a rich and detailed map of this journey of the Kundalini, the inner spiritual energy.

117. *aadhaar,* meaning *moolaadhaara,* or the root *chakra.* "inhalation" is *apaana vaayu.* "*manipura* complex" refers to *manipura chakra.*

118. *prana.*

119. Jnaneshwar calls it the *agni-chakra,* the chakra of fire, here. This is usually called the *ajna chakra.*

120. *sahasra-dala,* i.e., the *sahasrar.*

121. *brahma-randhra.*

122. This must be considered a sublime Shaktic or Shaivite hymn. The force of Maya is the power, *shakti,* of the supreme, the non-dual reality, that creates duality, the world. However, ultimately it does not create anything since the created universe is non-different from the supreme. This power of the ultimate itself guides the devotee to the supreme light.

123. Jnandev is using a classical metaphor for the illusory nature of the world.

124. Literally, "in the three worlds."

125. Listed in the text are *manas, buddhi, chitta,* and *antahkarana,* the traditional break-down of the mental instrument.

126. Jnaneshwar uses here the term *nirvana* to qualify Brahman.

127. *unmani.*

128. "Him" is literally *Brahman.*

129. Literally, "the knowledge of the Self."

These two lines could also mean, as DMS and PNJ

prefer, "don't associate with someone who has not seen the knowledge of the Self with his own eyes."

130. *turya,* the witness state of consciousness; see note 95.

131. "all" refers to the five elements.

132. "all" refers to the three worlds.

133. रसे, in DMS and PNJ.

134. The *ardha-matra* or half-syllable.

135. We have taken liberties here. The first two verses actually break down AUM, saying, "how do you see the half syllable that lives in A, enters U, and combines with M, and sits on top of the half syllable." A, U, and M represent the waking, dream and deep sleep states, and the crescent under the "M" in AUM, the half-syllable, the fourth or the *turya* state. Turya pervades all others.

We have translated "half-syllable" as "half-utterance" to represent its subtle nature. In the fourth line, Jnaneshwar talks about "the half-syllable on top of the half-syllable," probably meaning *turya-teeta,* beyond *turya.*

136. Literally, "and the great void is seen."

137. Literally, "seed of the void."

138. Truth-consciousness-bliss, the nature of Brahman.

139. The three *gunas* that form the universe.

140. More literally, "unapproachable by others."

141. *chidakash,* the space of consciousness.

142. "Speech, *para* (the transcendent speech) and otherwise."

143. Jnaneshwar seems to encapsulate, in two short verses, the whole theory of manifestation as Pratyabhijna philosophy would present it: the space of consciousness (which would be Shiva), contains the maiden, *Chiti Shakti,* who is the mother of the universe. She is one with all forms of speech, from *paraa vak* (transcendental speech) to *vaikahari,* gross speech. As *vaikhari,* she is cognate with creation. As *paraa vak,* she sits as the witness of all. See, e.g., *Pratyabhijna Hridyam* by Jaidev Singh, for the theory of creation according to Pratyabhijna.

144. *sa* and *ha* correspond to exhalation and inhalation; the subtle channels are the *ida* and *pingala.*

145. Representing the world.

146. Literally, "experience in your own body."

147. Jnaneshwar uses a curious construction here, which could probably be literally translated as: "Like the equal, the even, the one essence / see the Self pervading all / all that moves and doesn't."

148 The space of consciousness.

149. *Sat-chit-ananda.*

150. *anahata,* the heart chakra.

151. Muktabai was Jnaneshwar's sister. She holds "this knowledge."

152. "at the *brahma-randhra.*"

153. *ananda-svaroopa,* the form of bliss.

154. *nija-roopa,* form of the Self.

155. *chaitanya,* conscious.

156. "fortunate" is *sujaan,* one with a good life, or perhaps one with the right knowledge.

157. "great care" is *viveka,* discrimination.

158. Jnaneshwar uses the term *chitpada,* the state or station of consciousness.

As in many other poems, there is an exquisite melding of inquiry, epistemological insight, worship, and yogic process, all in this one poem, each process combining transparently with the other.

159. The text could perhaps also be translated as "*as* the flame," *jyoti.* However, based on the rest of the abhanga, "*through* the flame" makes more sense. As for the flame, see *Katha Upanishad,* "this being, like a smokeless flame, Lord of what was and what will be."

160. The flame's glory.

161. The text actually says, "all beings arise from the half-syllable," thus connecting the crescent-shaped half-syllable in *Om* back to Brahman which it represents. We feel justified in translating the "half-syllable" as "mere flicker" of the *jyoti.*

162. pure consciousness just beyond the darkness of deep sleep.

163. "play of the Self" is *atma-maya.* "Lord and his power" is *Shiva-Shakti.*

164. *chit-roopa,* the form of consciousness.

165. The text says only "the sky."

166. *pranava,* i.e., Om.

167. *moola-maya,* original illusion.

168. *brahma-randhra,* the inner opening into the *sahasrar,* the thousand-petalled lotus. See note 115.

169. There is an "undoubtedly" at the end of the first line of this couplet. It could go with either the first or the second line. We have assumed it goes with both.

170. The text says "How many get to see the form of *pranava* in this body?"

171 *unmani,* no-mind; *turya,* fourth-state.

172. *sa* and *ha* in the text, which stand for the inhalation and exhalation, or the external and the internal. A literal translation would be "He showed me the secret of the sounds of the letters *sa* and *ha.*"

173. *pranava,* the spirit, vitality, the Om.

174. *nada* and *bindu.*

175. *Brahma-jyoti.*

176. *prakriti, purusha; Shiva* and *Shakti.*

177. *unmani.*

178. See for example, *Kena Upanishad,* "He is the eye of the eye."

179. It could be "You are your own."

180. Literally, the last two lines are: "Lord of the great goddess/ you are your own/ all this conscious (*Chaitanya*) is in you."

181. Jnaneshwar says *auta-peetha,* Prakrit for *ajna* (or *agni,* as Jnaneshwar uses the term) *chakra,* the *chakra* between the eye-brows.

182. The four bodies are the gross, subtle, causal, and *turya* or fourth, corresponding to the four states of consciousness, waking, dream, deep sleep, and their witness.

183. *svaroopa,* own-nature or own-form.

184. *Brahman,* the Absolute.

185. Again, *auta-peetha,* or *ajna chakra* in Prakrit.

186. *trikuta,* the triangle in the *sahasrar.*

187. *ardha-matra,* half-syllable.

188. *shunya,* the void.

189. *unmani.*

190. *Brahman.*

191. See *Play of Consciousness* by Swami Muktananda for more about *blue,* the color of the conscious.

192. See also *Jnaneshwari* XVIII-25: "To say nothing is to praise you; to do nothing is to serve you; to be nothing is to be near you, in you."

193. The primal desire is to want to be something, do something, know something, say something.

Annotated Bibliography

Bhave, Vinoba. *Jnandevanchee Bhajane (with the Chintanika)*. Paonar, Wardha, India: Param Dham Prakashana, 2005.
Translations and contemplations on 150 of Jnaneshwar's abhangas. In Marathi.

Bhave, Vinoba. *Jnanoba Maooli*. Paonar, Wardha, India: Param Dham Prakashan, Sept 2014.
Essays on Jnaneshwar. In Marathi.

Bobde, P. V. *Garland of Divine Flowers: Selected Devotional Lyrics of Saint Jnaneshvara*. Delhi: Motilal Banarasidas, 1999.
Contains English prose translations of 110 of Jnaneshwar's poems, translated from P.N. Joshi's *Saartha Gaathaa*.

Chitre, Dilip. *Sri Jnandev's Anubhavamrut: The Immortal Experience of Being*. New Delhi: Sahitya Academi, 1996.
English translations of *Amritanubhava* in verse form.

Dandekar, S.V. and Mamasaheb. *Sartha Jnaneshwari*. Pune: Svananda Prakashan, 1973.
Our source for the verses from *Jnaneshwari*. This text has a comprehensive introduction to Jnaneshwar's philosophy and provides Marathi prose translation of the *Jnaneshwari*.

Das, Areyar and Mundra, Damodardas. *Jnanadev Chintanika*. Paonar, Wardha, India: Param Dham Prakashan, 1979.
Sanskrit and Hindi translations of Vinoba's *Jnandev Chintanika*. Sanskrit translated from Damodardas Mundra's Hindi translations.

Joshi, Kashinath Ananta, ed. *Sakala Sant Gaathaa, Vol I.* Pune: Sant Vangmaya Prakashan Mandir, 1975. The source for these translations, in Marathi.

Joshi, P.N. *Saartha Sri Jnandeva Abhanga Gaathaa*. Pune: Suvichar Prakashan, 1969.
Contains prose translations in contemporary Marathi of the abhangas in the Gaathaa.

Kanade, M.S., Nagarkar,. R.S. *Shri Jnandevancha Saartha Chikitsak Gaathaa*. Pune: Suvidya Prakashan, 1995.
In Marathi.

Kripananda, Swami. *Jnaneshwar's Gita: A rendering of the Jnaneshwari*. South Fallsburg: SYDA Foundation, 1999.
Rendering from Mr. Pradhan's translations.

Kulkarni, K. R. *Free rendering in verses of Changdeo-pasashti and other poems of Sant Jnaneshwar and Muktabai, with original text in Marathi.* Nagpur, India,1968 (Library of congress accession # PK2441.E3 K8).
Contains a translation into English of *Changdev Pasashti*, Jnandev's *Hari Path*, and Muktabai's *taatee* abhangas.

Macnicol, Nicol. *Psalms of Maratha Saints: One hundred and eight Hymns translated from the Marathi*. Calcutta: Association Press, 1919.
Perhaps the first English translations of Jnaneshwar's poems. Contains translations of four of his abhangas.

Muktananda, Swami. *Play of Consciousness.* South Fallsburg, NY: SYDA Foundation, 2000.

Patil, H.A. *Shri Sant Jnaneshwar yanchee Sartha Gaathaa,* Mumukshu Paathashaalaa, Pandharpur. 2010.
A lot of this work is a direct or near-direct copy of *Shree Jnaneshwar Maharaj Saartha Gaathaa* by Dada Maharaj Sakhare.

Pradhan, V. G. *Jnaneshwari: A Song Sermon on the Bhagavadgita,* Volumes I and II, edited by H.M. Lambert. Bombay: Blackie & Son Publishers, 1969.

Prakashan, Vamanraj. *Baapa Rakhuma Devivaru*. Pune, India.
Monthly publication dedicated to the literature and knowledge of Jnaneshwar. In Marathi.

Ramana Maharshi. *The Spiritual Teaching of Ramana Maharshi*. Shambhala Press, 1988.

Ranade, R. D. *Mysticism in India: The Poet-Saints of Maharashtra*. Albany: SUNY Press, 1985.
Contains a section with excerpts from Jnaneshwar's abhangas.

Ranade, R.D. *Jnaneshwar, the Guru's Guru*. New York: SUNY Press, 1994.

Sakhare, Dada Maharaj. *Shree Jnaneshwar Maharaj Saartha Gaathaa*. Pune, Alandi: Yashodhan Prakashan, 1995.
Contains prose translations in contemporary Marathi of all the abhangas in the Gaathaa.

Schelling, Andrew, ed. *Love and the Turning Seasons: India's Poetry of Spiritual and Erotic Longing*. Berkeley: Counterpoint Press, 2014.
Contains three poems by Jnaneshwar translated into English by Dilip Chitre.

Singh, Jaideva. *Spanda Karikas*. Delhi: Motilal Banarasidass, 1980.

Singh, Jaideva. *Pratyabhijnahrdayam: The Secret of Self-recognition*. Delhi: Motilal Banarasidass, 1980.

Singh, Jaidev. *Siva Sutra: The Yoga of Supreme Identity*. Delhi: Motilal Banarasidas, 1979.

Svaroopananda, Swami. *Shrimat Abhang Jnaneshwari.* Pawas, Ratnagiri: Swami Svaroopananda Seva Mandal, 1960. Two volumes. Rendering of *Jnaneshwari* in more modern Marathi in Ovi Meter.

Adventure of Consciousness

6

- Analytical Ayurveda/ Dr. K.A. Latheef
- Upaniṣads and Edith Stein: *A Dialogue on Models of The Person/* Thomas Marottipparyail
- Tirthaṅkarāsana: *A Work on Jaina Yoga/* Shantilal D. Parakh
- Aparokṣānubhūti: *The Essence of Self Realization/* Dr. Shrikrishn Deshmukh
- A Critical Study in the Schism in Early Buddhist Monastic Tradition: *Dasavatthu and Pañcavatthu/* Lokananda C. Bhikkhu
- Mystical Poems of Jnaneshwar: *Original Translations from the Marathi/* Anand Mundra

INDIAN KAVYA LITERATURE (8 Vols.)

A.K. Warder

Vol. I : Literary Criticism presents Indian Literary Criticism including the aesthetic theories about the nature of enjoyment of literature, the techniques of dramaturgy and poetics, the nature of the literary genres and a sketch of the milieu of the writers and critics.
(xx+294p) biblio., index **[978-81-208-0446-3]**

Vol. II : Origins and Formation of the Classical Kavya deal with the classical model created by Valmiki, Gunadhya, Asvaghese Satavahana and others.
(vi+405p) append., index **[978-81-208-0447-0]**

Vol. III : Early Medieval Period presents the celebrated writers like Sudraka, Visnusarman, Kalidasa, Pravarasena, Amaruka, Bharavi, Subandhu and Visakhadatta, with a new analysis and appreciation of their poetry.
(307p) append., index (In Press) **[978-81-208-0448-7]**

Vol. IV : The Ways of Originality describes in more detail the extensive literature preserved from the 7th and 8th centuries. It analyses the extant novels of famous writers such as Bana, Dandin, Kutuhala Haribhadra and Uddyotana. The plays of Harsa, Narayana, and Bhavabhuti are also assessed critically.
(xii+641p) biblio., notes, ref. **[978-81-208-0449-4]**

Vol. V : The Bold Style (Saktibhadra to Dhanapala)
(xiii+891p) index (In Press) **[978-81-208-0450-0]**

Vol. VI : The Art of Storytelling continues the exploration of Indian Literature (Kavya) into the eleventh century, from Padmagupta and Atula to Bilhana and Manovinoda.
(xiii+852p) biblio, index (In Press) **[978-81-208-0615-3]**

Vol. VII : The Wheel of Time (2 Pts.) presents The Indian Literature of 12th & 13th centuries History.
(2 Parts) (xiv, vi+1114p) biblio, index **[978-81-208-2028-9] (Set)**

Vol. VIII : The Performance of Kavya in the+14 details the performance in the streets and on stages, especially in theatres, where kayva flourished everywhere to the south, also in Mithila and Nepala in 14th century and later period.
(xiv+421p), biblio., index **[978-81-208-3448-4]**

THE POETIC LIGHT (2 Vols.)

(Kavyaprakasha of Mammata) Text with Translation and Sampradayaprakasini of Srividyacakravartin with complete comment Sanketa of Ruyyaka

Ed. and Tr. by ***R.C. Dwivedi***

Delhi, 1977, Vol. I: Ullasas, I-VI; Vol. II: Ullasas VII-X; (xv+iv+10+591p.), demy octavo, abbrev., biblio., index, notes

[978-81-208-0080-X]

[978-81-208-0099-7]

WORKS OF KALIDASA (2 Vols.)

—Edited with an Exhaustive Introduction, Translation, and Critical Explanatory notes by *C.R. Devadhar*

Kalidasa is well-known for his dramatic and poetic compositions.

Volume 1 The Three Dramas: Abhijnana-Sakuntalam, Vikramorvasiya and Mala-vikagnimitram

Volume 2 The Five Kavyas. Srngaratilaka, Rtusamhara, Meghadutam, Kumara-sambhava and Raghuvamsam.

Delhi, 2016 (Rep.), crown octavo, Vol. I **Dramas** *(lx, 965p.)*
[978-81-208-0023-6]

Delhi, 2016 (Rep.) crown octavo, Vol. II **Poetry** *(xxxvii+1440p), append., notes*
[978-81-208-0024-3]

Performing Arts

NEW AGE MUSIC

Music for Mind, Body & Spirit

INSTRUMENTAL MUSIC CDs ONLY

1. **BEYOND WORLDS**—*Michael Wild* (Instrumental/62 Minutes/1CD)
2. **BREATHING RHYTHMS**—*Glen Velez* (Music/55 Minutes • 9-pages study guide/1CD)
3. **CAROLINE MYSS' CHAKRA MEDITATION MUSIC**—*Stevin McNamara* (Music/73 Minutes/1 CD • 21-pages study guide)
4. **CELESTIAL SOUNDS** —*Michael Wild* (Instrumental /65 Minutes/1CD)
5. **CELTIA**—*Mark Winterborne* (Instrumental/64 Minutes/1CD)
6. **CELTIC MEDITATION MUSIC** —*Aine Minogue* (Instrumental/ 70 Minutes/1CD)
7. **CHANTING THE CHAKRA**—*Layne Redmond* (Music/46 Minutes/1CD • 24 pages study guide)
8. **DANCING LOTUS**—*Bapu Padmanabha* (Instrumental/53 Minutes/1CD)
9. **DOLPHIN FANTASY**—*Nicholas Dodd* (Instrumental/65 Minutes/1CD)
10. **DRUM**—*Geoff Johns* (Instrumental/71 Minutes/1CD)
11. **ECHOES OF THE SPIRIT**—*Gentle Thunder* (Instrumental/52.37 Minutes/1CD)
12. **EYE OF THE WOLF**—*Medwyn Goodall* (Instrumental/45 Minutes/1CD)
13. **FREE SPIRIT**—*Christopher Buckman* (Instrumental/60 Minutes/1CD)
14. **HANDS OF GOLD** —*Amrita* (Instrumental 59 Minutes/1CD)
15. **HIMALAYAN NIGHTS** Sitar and Tabla Backgrounds for Relaxation—*Agni & Lewis Howard* (Instrumental/59 Minutes/1CD)
16. **HIMALAYAN SUNRISE** Sitar and Tabla Backgrounds for Vitality—*Agni & Lewis Howard* (Instrumental/60 Minutes/1CD)
17. **HIMALAYAN TOUCH** Sitar and Tabla Backgrounds for Healing—*Agni & Lewis Howard* (Instrumental/63 Minutes/1CD
18. **HOPE** —*Padmanabha Bapu* (Instrumental/ 74 Minutes/1CD)
19. **I, OMAR** —*Donald Walters* (Music/ 61 Minutes/1CD)
20. **ILLUSIONS**—*Padmanabha Bapu* (Instrumental/56 Minutes/1CD)
21. **LAND OF THE INCA**—*Medwyn Goodall* (Instrumental/52.37 Minutes/1CD)
22. **LET GO**—*Padmanabha Bapu* (Instrumental/72 Minutes/1CD)
23. **LUCID DREAMER**—*Paul Lawler* (Instrumental/50.36 Minutes/1CD)
24. **MANTRAS FROM DAWN TO DUSK**—*Nilesh D. Nathwani* (Instrumental/67 Minutes/1CD)
25. **MASSAGE MUSIC (Vol. I & II)**—*Amrita* (Instrumental/74 Minutes/2CDs) **(Vol.1&2)**
26. **MEDITATION WITH BAMBOOS**—*Padmanabha Bapu* (Instrumental/74 Minutes/1CD)
27. **MUSIC FOR RELAXING (Vol. I)**—*Amrita* (Instrumental 65 Minutes/1CD)
28. **MUSIC FOR RELAXING (Vol. 2)**—*David Mcgerty* (Instrumental 57 Minutes/1CD)
29. **MUSIC TO AWAKEN SUPERCONSCIOUSNESS** —*Donald Walters* (Instrumental 65 Minutes/1CD)
30. **THE MYSTIC HARP (Vol. I)**—*Derek Bell* (Instrumental/70 Minutes/1CD)
31. **THE MYSTIC HARP (Vol. II)**—*Derek Bell* (Instrumental/72 Minutes/1CD)
32. **OCEAN DAWN**—*Amrita* (Instrumental 58 Minutes/1CD)
33. **PACHELBELS CANON**—*Christopher Buckman* (Instrumental/ 45 Minutes/1CD)
34. **RHYTHMS OF THE CHAKRAS**—*Glen Velez* (Music/ 52 Minutes/1CD •10 pages study guide)
35. **SECRETS OF LOVE:** Melodies to Open Your Heart—*Donald Walters* (Instrumental/70 Minutes/1CD)
36. **SHAKUHACHI MEDITATION MUSIC** —*Stan Richardson* (Music/142 Minutes/2CDs)
37. **SLEEP SOUND**—*Amrita* (Instrumental/61 Minutes/1CD)
38. **SOLO TABLA**—*Robert Gottlieb* (Instrumental/120 Minutes/2CDs)
39. **STAR DREAMS**—*Michael Wild* (Instrumental/61 Minutes/1CD)
40. **STILLNESS**—*Padmanabha Bapu* (Instrumental/70 Minutes/1CD)
41. **TAI CHI**—*Amrita* (Instrumental/61 Minutes/1CD)
42. **THE ESSENTIAL KAMASUTRA**—*Wendy Doniger* (Spoken-Word Audio • 150 Minutes/2CDs)
43. **UNIVERSAL LOVE** —*Nawang Khechog* (Music/75 Minutes/1CD)
44. **WAVES**—*Nicholas Dodd* (Instrumental/42 Minutes/1CD)
45. **WHISPERS TO THE MIND**—*Amrita* (Instrumental/61 Minutes/1CD)
46. **ZEN GARDEN**—*Amrita* (Instrumental/61 Minutes/1CD)